VOICES of
STANLEY

VOICES *of*
STANLEY

JO BATH

The
History
Press

For Paul, Richard and Mike,
who kept me sane(ish).

First published 2014

The History Press
The Mill, Brimscombe Port
Stroud, Gloucestershire, GL5 2QG
www.thehistorypress.co.uk

© Jo Bath, 2014

The right of Jo Bath to be identified as the Author
of this work has been asserted in accordance with the
Copyright, Designs and Patents Act 1988.

British Library Cataloguing in Publication Data.
A catalogue record for this book is available from the British Library.

ISBN 978 0 7524 6037 6

Typesetting and origination by The History Press
Printed in Great Britain

CONTENTS

ACKNOWLEDGEMENTS

Voices of Stanley is drawn from the extensive and fascinating collections of Beamish, the Living Museum of the North. Without the museum's dedication to the collection and preservation of interviews, photographs and archive material of north-eastern life, sustained for over forty years, this book could not have been written. My thanks go in particular to Paul Castrey.

I would also like to thank Northumbria Police, who came to my rescue when a draft of this book was stolen. Sadly they could not recover my work, but they did show me every consideration and they did catch the thieves.

Most of all, my thanks go out to all those men and women who, between 1974 and 2010, sat down with an audio recorder to leave for posterity such vivid glimpses into life in the pit villages of northern County Durham.

INTRODUCTION

For reasons of space and clarity it has been necessary to edit some of the memories presented here, but I have done this with as light a hand as possible, to allow the interviewees' own personal stories to shine through. Still, something is lost in the transcription of the spoken interview to the written book, not least of which is the distinctive accent of the region.

In the first half of the twentieth century, Stanley stood at the heart of a network of villages dominated by, and often built to house the workforce of, the coal-mining industry. In the memories that follow, the influence of the pits shows up in all sorts of ways, obvious and subtle. And since the mines' closure, the world they supported – with its pit buzzers and poss tubs, jarping and netties – is gradually passing out of memory. This book represents a small window into that world.

Jo Bath, 2014

One

DOMESTIC WORK

King, Queen and Boss

Mother was king, queen, boss; yes, the whole lot. My father was the wage earner, the supplier of money. He was always in the background, always there, very important – if he wasn't at work, of course. If ever we hurt ourselves it was to mum we went, and if we had to be punished, it was mother – I've never heard my father raise his voice towards me, to any of us in fact.

Ernie Cheeseman

Five to Look After

Mother had five to look after: she had five pairs of boots to get clean every morning for us to get off to school, and for the two girls she had to put their hair in ringlets hanging down their neck. There was a lot of fighting; they had a job to separate us when we were younger. We had to be in at eight o'clock on a night, if we were in a minute after eight father would take his cap off and clout you cross the back of the neck.

Jack Edgell

The Chancellor of the Exchequer

The woman was the master as well as the mistress of the house. The poor old miner, considering the amount of work he had to do hewing coal, was only a wage-getter. The Chancellor of the Exchequer, all that sort of thing, that was the woman of the house, his wife. She would make the meal, and she would put the meal on the table. No one but no one was allowed to touch that meal until the

Amateur photographer Mr Watson with his family. Mr Watson, from South Moor, took pictures of Edwardian Stanley and also took a photographic booth to local fairs and galas.

miner himself had had his fill, then what he left the family could have. Nowadays that seems terrible, but look at it this way, if he didn't eat to gain energy, if he didn't keep his health, he couldn't go to work and nobody ate.

Ernie Cheeseman

Bacon for the Pitman

A pitman hadn't a good feed for his breakfast if he didn't get bacon on the morning, a good fry of bacon. It used to be pretty thick, there was lovely dripping out of it – they used to dip the kids bread in it and things like that. At Christmastime you would save the goose dripping and spread that on your bread just the same as butter. And if lads run a message for anybody, when they came back they would be asked, 'Would you like a slice of jam and bread?' They were glad of a slice of jam and bread, or a slice of dripping bread, people hadn't money to give them you see.

Jack Edgell

The Kitchen Range

We had the coal fire and we'd open up the boiler, and that fire did everything. My mother used to bake, and on the fireside you'd see about eight loaf tins when she was doing the baking; and that went on in every miner's home. And in the oven there would be some dinner, and on the side would be the big end boiler where she boiled the water for us to get washed. When there was nobody to get washed then we used to keep this side boiler full of water every day. My mother would fill the large iron pan with broth and that broth would be used two or three times in a week, so really them big, black pans made a lot of broth and they lasted a family for quite a while.

Samuel Jackson

First World War Rations

My mother used to make potatoes and turnips and meat, but you didn't get much meat you know. She said, 'Well I'll make a pie with that,' and everybody got a decent share in the pie dish. Put some carrots in or peas or something like that, nice. And of course when you wanted tea you could always guarantee it was jam,

Here, Beamish Museum has recreated the interior of a pit cottage from around 1913.

that's all you would get. Or a bit of bread and cheese. You didn't grumble, you just carried on, made the most of things.

Joseph French

Onions Seven Days a Week

My father had moved with the pit closing down and we were left and the neighbours looked after us. My father was sending them money every week to buy us grub. And we had onions for breakfast, onions for dinner, onions for tea and onions for supper: fried, boiled, any way. My father had been away about a month when he got a weekend home. And he came home and he said, 'Everything alright?' And before he could say anything else I said, 'It would be if we could get anything other than onions to eat! We've had nowt but onions – breakfast, dinner, tea and supper – onions! Onions every day, seven days a week! I'm sick of bloody onions!' My father went mad – he'd been sending them two pounds a week, something like that, which was a hell of a lot of money in those days. And they were living off the fat of the land and were feeding us onions out of the allotment. And my father said, 'That's it! I'll have you away from here!' And within a fortnight we were on the back of a wagon on our way to Billingham.

Anonymous

Fruit and Veg

My mother used to make all her own jams and chutneys and pickles. There was a garden where we had all our vegetables – potatoes, turnips and carrots and parsnips and celery and leeks. My mother always had a fruit basket in the pantry, there'd be apples and oranges and plums. We would always get something to take to school.

R. Powton

Stotty Cakes

I used to walk from the school and at the house at the end of the terrace, Eden Terrace, there was a woman called Mrs Burns. She had a family of a lot of boys, and often she used to be baking stotty cakes. Just out the window there was sort of a grill thing, and she used to put them outside to cool. And sometimes she'd say to me, 'Would you like a bit of stotty cake, Hinnie?' And she'd go and put some margarine or whatever it was on it, and hand me this piece of stotty cake.

Irene Wilson

Baking Day

Wednesday was baking day. The house was filled with lovely smells of freshly baked bread. My mother used to bake for the four of us. After kneading for a little while, there would be a spotless clean towel put over it allowing it to rise, and then it would be cut into small portions and put into tins, which would be put along the steel fender in front of the fire to let it rise a little bit further. You could tell when the oven became a proper temperature by opening the oven door and putting your elbow in – or get some flour and sprinkle it on the steel shelves in the oven and the different hues of brown would tell you if it was the right temperature for pastry or what have you. So the bread would be put into the oven and brought out and put on the backyard wall to cool off. There was a little bit of dough left and if we were at home we would make different shapes – men and what have you. Every house had an earthenware jar in the coldest part of the pantry with a towel over it to keep the bread fresh. It was always a treat to come running home from school on baking day and get a fresh slice of bread with occasionally butter, but more often than not margarine, lovely margarine, and a whacking great dollop of jam. It was beautiful!

Ernie Cheeseman

Thursday Baking

Nearly all Hobson village baked on a Thursday, and it was a delight – in fact the minister used to like to come on a Thursday because there was always a lovely tea, straight out of the oven. There would be brown bread and white bread and teacakes and scones and sandwich cakes, and always a fruit tart of some description. My mother used to make macaroons with jam and coconut on the top, and that would last us a week.

R. Powton

Sunday Dinner

Mother would seldom go to chapel on Sunday morning because there was the Sunday dinner to prepare. If we were ill and stayed home on a Sunday morning the smell of mothballs slowly changed to the delicious smell of roast beef. The Yorkshire pudding was the highlight of the Sunday dinner: the highlight of the week, culinary speaking.

Ernie Cheeseman

Ploating Chickens

I remember as a girl, Mrs Hobbsby asked my mother if she would help her ploat all these fowl – ducks and chickens and turkeys. So mum said she would, and of course mother says, 'You can come with me; you can pick the feathers up and put them in the bag' – you always had to do something in those days. They would sit in this big room and it was very cold, and ploat these ducks and hens. They were for sale; local people always ordered their fowl from the local farmer you see.

Ethel Murray

Ginger Beer

On Thursdays in our house my mother would brew ginger beer in a huge basin. If it was thundering my mother would say, 'Oh dear, it will make my beer go flat!' She would bottle it and on a Thursday morning before we went to chapel people would come and buy a bottle of ginger beer for a penny. A penny was quite something in those days, and that went towards the finances of the house, because we weren't well-off money wise.

Ernie Cheeseman

There Wasn't a Thing Wasted

Miners worked hard but they also ate well to keep up the energy. It was all energy-giving stuff: suet puddings, dumplings, mince meat, pie meat, stews – sheep's heads, beast's cheek. There wasn't a thing wasted, cow heel, tripes. Monday was a day for killing and getting meat at the shop. On a Tuesday it was sausages, minced meat, a few chops. On the Wednesday it was pie meat and stewing steak, tatty pots, pot pies, meat in the cloth. All stodgy food, plenty of suet in, plenty of kidney. You could sell every bit of dripping. They used to get big chunks of dripping because they didn't use cooking oil. They used beef dripping for chips. Friday was usually fish day. Of course the Catholics wouldn't eat meat on a Friday. And on a Saturday it was back to the joint.

Mr Wears

Christmas Cake and Rice Cake

My grandfather kept hens so we always had a cock chicken for Christmas, which in those days was a luxury. My grandmother always made my mother a Christmas

Demonstrators baking pies in Foulbridge Colliery Cottage, Beamish Museum.

cake and a rice cake, she would never give her the recipe for the cake but she always provided them. We were a lot luckier than most people.

Iris Summers

Wash Day

On washing day the house was filled full of steam and smelling of ammonia and blue mottled soap. Believe me, the muscles my mother must have had to scrub. How did the woman get her whites white? With hard work and dolly blue. If the household had girls their underwear would always be done in Lux Flakes, whereas the pit shirts would be mottle blue. It was just one step away from caustic soda. It would take the skin off you! But they were very dirty, and they used to get them white. We had a mangle as well. You changed the gear and you turned the handle – that was always my job. And this would be going round and around, and horizontally rather than vertically washing the clothes. Then you would take the clothes out and change the gear for the rollers and squeeze the water out and you would put them on the table and further scrub them.

Ernie Cheeseman

Dirty Overalls

Overalls really did get greasy. If you took them home to be washed in the washer, you had to wash the washer out afterwards. So you'd just smack them against the wall, or stand them in a pail of water with this degreaser stuff you used to get at the pits, like some sort of acid, and leave them in there and then hang them out to dry.

John and Eddie Nicholson

Dadding

Understand that when you are bringing coal into the house for the fire you are bringing muck into the house. There was no pit head baths. My father would take his boots off at the door; he would undress in front of the fire. His clothes would be full of dust and they would be carefully picked up and 'dadded' against the wall – bang the dust out against the backyard wall. That was a joke as well, 'Me wife's gone and dadded me pit watch again!' It must have happened once or twice.

Ernie Cheeseman

Mother's Sewing

Mother used to do an awful lot of sewing. She used to wash once a fortnight, and the next week she would sew. She used to make petticoats, nightdresses, shirts, dresses for us to go to school, pinafores and aprons, pillowcases, foot bases for round the bottom of the bed. And quilts. She hemmed all the sheets, all the tea towels, and she used to sew for my grandmother too.

R. Powton

Ironing

On Tuesday the irons were put on the fire. It's no use putting your irons in a smoky fire, it had to be built up, get all the blackness off the fire. Then you could put your irons close to the fire otherwise you've got all your hard work with a soot mark. There were different shaped irons. My mother just had the inverted heart shape. There were others, of course, which were probably not so good. They would open up the iron and take out the cast-iron part inside and put it in the fire and when it was red hot put it back in there and close it up. But if you were the colliery manager's wife you would have a gas iron.

Ernie Cheeseman

Shoes

When you got shoes you had to take care of them, not gan kicking this and kicking that you know. Mostly people used to buy clogs. They were only half a crown a pair, and they were warm. I used to get some little short cobblers' nails and I used to buy the leather, cut it and nail it on and that saved it for quite a long while.

Joseph French

Shoe Mending

My dad used to mend all the shoes in the house. He used to go to Stevenson's down the moor, buy a bit of leather for one and six, bring it back and he would sole the shoes. I had a pair of football boots with studs in, he took them out and I went to school in them boots.

Derek Hall

Bath Water

I can recollect my Uncle Joe – who lived up at Beamish – coming in and sitting in the bath and my Aunt Bertha washing his back and the water turning black and soapy, and the little Labrador dog coming and drinking it when my Uncle Joe was in the bath!

John Nicholson

Tin Bath

Father would kneel at the bath and wash his top half. He would strip right down to his pit hoggers (they were ordinary trousers but cut off very short), and he would sit on a cracket and put his feet in and wash up to the bottom of his hoggers. He wouldn't wash his private parts whilst there was people around and so it would probably be once a week when no one was in the house.

Ernie Cheeseman

A member of staff at Beamish Museum about to demonstrate a traditional bath, 1983.

Old-Fashioned Dressing Table

At Beamish Hall they were all four-poster beds and every bed had a commode at the side and there was like a little step. There was two steps, you know, and the middle one pulled out and that was the potty. And that was a step to get into bed – they were so high! And there were old-fashioned dressing tables, wash stands with a bowl and jug, and you put your brass can of water in. The towels were over the top to keep them warm. We carried water often – they had to have their hands washed for midday lunch, and for the four o'clock afternoon tea, and then at half past seven at night. Then you'd to go round every time they'd been in their room, you had to go round with your slop bucket and your towels, wash all these basins out, collect the cans, empty the potties, sweep the hearth, oh it was constant!

Minnie Arbuckle

Black Leading

Friday morning was filled full of metal polish and black lead, because that was the time that mother cleaned the huge iron kitchen range. Ours was all stamped, you know, with a bull's head cast in it. And it was made absolutely beautiful and all the fire irons, the steel fender, all had to be silver steel-looking, and all the brass had to be brilliant. That was a whole morning and mam would be getting the Friday dinner ready looking like a pitman, all smudges and what have you.

Ernie Cheeseman

The Kitchen Maid

Mary Cassidy was the kitchen maid. She wasn't the height of the table. She used to put her bucket up on the top of the table, and she got on top and started to scrub, crawling down it until she reached the end, and then she jumped off. She was funny, Mary Cassidy.

Minnie Arbuckle

Mothballs

The beds were done on a Thursday and that's where you would get smells, from packets of dried lavender and things like that mixed, strangely, with camphor balls and mothballs. But the beds would be done. Mind you, a Thursday was when the Co-op delivered the groceries, so you couldn't be upstairs doing the beds when the grocer man came.

Ernie Cheeseman

Annfield Plain Wooden Houses

In Annfield Plain there were wooden houses. They were very basic houses. They had two bedrooms, a main kitchen, the coalhouse was outside, and of course a very small pantry, with a little wooden shutter. What I remember mostly about the house was it was very dark. The lustres that would be on the mantelpiece were always attractive to youngsters, ruby-coloured and jingling. You had to be quiet when grandfather shaved, you daren't move when he was shaving, because he was shaving with a cut-throat razor. So although usually a quiet man, I'm afraid he did get moments when if anyone spoke they would be chastised.

Jim Kay

Brass on the Mantelpiece

Wood mantelpieces, about six foot six, we used to make those and have them draped with frames right around those mantelpieces, with a line on for the pitmen to put their socks on and their body shirts when they came from the pit, to dry them you see. And all the brasses came off the mantelpiece on the Friday morning, they were put onto the table and cleaned, and they were put back onto the mantelpiece on the Saturday morning for the weekend, then they just stopped there all the week. But the next Friday off they came again onto the table and cleaned.

Jack Edgell

Making Clippy Mats

Mother was trained as a dressmaker, and she used to make a lot of our clothes, and very good clothes they were. One of the nicest, which would be termed a jacket now – we called it a jerkin – was made out of a black overcoat someone had. She made me a jerkin with a zip on, and it had some patch pockets. I thought it was great. Like lots of women she made clippy mats as well. Her and my dad would write the pattern out on the mats, and use some frames which would stretch from one corner of the room to the other depending on the size of the mat. Any old clothes were made into clippings and kept in a bag. We used to cut the clippings and me mother would sort out the colours. If she wasn't doing anything in particular we would get the mat frames out, they would lie across the backs of the chairs and you would sit hour after hour making clippy mats.

John Nicholson

Blacklocks

Do you remember blacklocks? We had a sitting room and I remember not putting the light on and standing on one without my slippers, squash. I set off such a scream – I think I was about ten year old then, mother had to come and lift me up. I was petrified, I couldn't move, standing on this blacklock. And we used to have all the beetles in the sink. Mother would get the boiling kettle and pour it, and scald them all, then take a shovel and take them out.

Doreen Scarrat

Beetles in the Cupboard

At Eden Place, when I first went there, in the cupboard next to the fire there was beetles that big. I always pass the joke that the bugger was trying my pit boots on one morning when I got up. Beetles, there was millions and millions. Ma said, 'That cupboard'll have to come out!' We took that cupboard out next to the fireplace – what a hell of a difference it made. But they weren't all gone mind, afore we left. There were some still there.

Bob Barker

Children's Chores

I had to bring two scuttles of coal in from the coalhouse before I went to school, and then some more when I came in from school. And I used to paint the garage every year in the Easter holidays with this black tarry substance. I used to get covered in the stuff as well, filthy black tar. Grandma's pension, every Thursday, I used to get that. My grandmother's brother-in-law, he needed a doctor's certificate to get some pension for cataracts, severe cataracts – he could hardly see – so I had to go and sit in the doctor's queue every week to get his certificate. He never gave me anything, miserable old devil.

John Williamson

Senna Pods

Epsom salts and castor oil, that's what you used to get. Mother gave us senna pods. There was five of us around the table and we all had them in a little cup, you know; we used to put raisins in to make them better to eat. When mother weren't watching we used to sometimes pour it into the younger ones, then she'd come and say, 'You haven't supped that already? What were you doing with it?' and the younger ones would say, 'We've got it! He's put it in my cup!' Castor oil, she used to nip your nose and open your mouth.

Jack Edgell

Castor Oil

If we were bad, we'd have a dose of castor oil, or olive oil, or some sort of ginger tea if we had a tummy ache. Mother used to get a bottle of little peppermints, very, very small, from the chemist. She used to give us two or three drops in a cup if we were poorly. We never knew for us to go to the doctors. Mother got a dose of castor oil and we stopped off a day of school for fear we did any damage in the schoolyard, when we maybe had to run to the toilet!

Eliza Brown

Very Good with Soap

If we had blood poisoning or anything like that, there was an old lady at the end of the street; she was very good with soap. She would rub the soap into the wound and you weren't long in being put right, you know. If there was anybody ill, we used to send for the midwives, they didn't only go to confinements. They were still very good; there was a lot of credit due to them.

Jack Edgell

Mrs Lorimer was well known in Holmside and Beamish as the unofficial midwife, *c.* 1900.

Moving House

In them days, when you moved house you hadn't many belongings, and it was on a little flat cart, and men with caps on. Mother was carrying me, trying to keep up with this man that had all our possessions, trying to get there with the key to let him in. She put me on the doorstep to open the door. She opened the door and I walked along the passage – they didn't know I could walk, I'd never walked a step before! Me father said, 'I told you that bairn was going to bring us luck.' So I was the first foot inside the house.

Mrs Linsley

Work in Domestic Service

We had our breakfast, and then they had theirs. Then we were upstairs, doing the bedrooms and cleaning. I had fireplaces to do, and the baths to scrub, and the bathroom floor to do. And carrying up coal – we had those great big scuttles like a fireman's helmet, huge things, they must have held about a hundredweight of coal. You had your housemaid's box, with your little brushes, and your sweeping, and your dusters and things and that got lifted off, and you put your ashes and things in the bottom. And you had that in one hand, and a big coal bucket in the other.

Minnie Arbuckle

Dess Beds and Straw

You've heard about the Dess bed, haven't you? You open the Dess bed out and this iron frame lets down. Some of the family were upstairs, and the parents would have the youngest children downstairs with them sleeping in that Dess bed … it's surprising how they managed. The whole family would be spread out either upstairs or downstairs and there was a lot of mixed people in those beds upstairs – in fact they went on until well into the teens before they really got separated.

My sisters and my mother used to sleep downstairs and my father and my brother and I used to sleep upstairs. The mattresses were straw – our first ones were straw, then we managed to get a feather one after that. Some days we used to put overcoats (and a woollen hat on) over the top of the blankets hat during the bad weather.

Samuel Jackson

Two Beamish Hall maids.

Margaret Ann (Purdy) Porter, housekeeper at Langley Moor Farm, Annfield Plain, collecting water with buckets on a yoke, 1938.

Hot Water Bottles

We had some hot water bottles which we filled with sand. We also used to have a firebrick which would go in the oven. We used to have an old sock and would put the firebrick in that. And if the sock got a hole in it, when your foot touched that, you used to knee yourself under the chin!

John Nicholson

Bedtime Preparations

When they were in having their eight o'clock meal, we had to go round and turn all the bedspreads down and all the pillows fluffed up. And an easy chair pulled towards the fireplace, and a dressing gown laid out, and a nightdress laid out, and a stool with their slippers on.

Minnie Arbuckle

Two

HOME LIFE

Grandfather

My grandfather couldn't read or write, so he would play a lot of 'patience' type games. There were puzzles like connecting and disconnecting peculiar bent pieces of wire. I always remember when I was taken up there on a Saturday afternoon I was ushered into his bedroom – because he became bedridden, you see, and this magnificent six foot six man didn't look fat but he was huge. He had a beard and sort of awe-inspiring voice. He would say, 'Bring the lad to me,' and my mother would usher me up in front of him. With great ceremony he would reach to the bedside table, open a packet and I had either a black bullet or a Tyne mint, which of course was great and that was him showing his love for me as it were.

Ernie Cheeseman

Clothing

When I was a laddy, I had short buttoned cords, they were the main trousers. I used to fasten them below the knee. And they were quite warm, and then the jersey, dark blue jersey with a rubber collar, and my cap you see, that's all you had. And a little overcoat to put on. Suits them days was very cheap, if you had the money to buy them, and you would get a suit when you were sort of older. And they were thirty shilling a buy, in a good suit you looked smart right up to the time you got married.

Joseph French

Three bachelor brothers from Annfield Plain enjoy playing a game in 1937. (*Durham Advertiser*)

The Parlour

Mother had a billiard table in the parlour. We used to get our pals in, the girls, and we used to be dressing dolls and mother would give us all the bits of materials that she had, that she could cut off of old things. Old pinneys or anything, you know, to make doll's clothing.

Eliza Brown

Making Paste Eggs

Everyone of my generation knows exactly what I mean by a paste egg. Now a lot of women used to save their onion peel skin, and they would put it in a pan with some water. Each egg had its own little bag and was placed in the pan with warm water with as much onion peel as you could get in there, and you would boil them for seven to ten minutes. The dye out of the onion skin would be sort of filtered through the canvas bag and wonderful patterns used to come out. There was great pride in this but if some woman said, 'Oh, I'm too busy doing housework' you could put a couple of spoonfuls of Camp coffee and of course you've got a brown egg and that's it. Before you did anything else with the egg you would get a candle and write on the egg, or draw designs, flowers and so on. The dye wouldn't take on the wax and there would be no argument over whose egg was which.

Ernie Cheeseman

Celebrating Christmas

The week before Christmas, everybody used to have Christmas trees. We used to leave the door open and anybody could come in, and then of course we used to go round and see who had the biggest one and who we thought had the nicest one. Christmastime there was always a social evening at the chapel – another supper, and of course for the younger ones there would be Postman's Knock and that sort of thing. We would go home between eight and nine because Santa Claus was going to come and he wouldn't be there until after the singers had been.

R. Powton

Stocking Fillers

You would get an orange in a stocking, maybe some sweets and a gazoo; it was like a little submarine, it just blew one note. A lot of our presents were home-made, my dad made a rifle. The joiner would make the stock and my dad was a blacksmith so he would make the barrel and the trigger mechanism. They would probably be making a few when the boss wasn't looking, knocking out these things for Christmas.

Eddie and John Nicholson

White Candy Mice

We made our own decorations at Christmas with crêpe paper – we didn't have a Christmas tree but we had what we called mistletoe, which was two hoops covered in crêpe paper with the ornaments hanging from it and it hung from the ceiling. We didn't get a lot of presents but we always got something, a book or a doll and an apple, orange, nuts and little white candy mice or a pig or something like that.

Iris Summers

The back of this card reads, 'This is Father Christmas who has just come down to the infant school wishing you a Merry Christmas'.

Christmas in the Strike

I always remember the 1926 Christmas. I was told in no uncertain manner by my mother, 'There will be no Father Christmas this Christmas,' because there was no money. Now I was nine years old, I was at that stage where I'm thinking, is there a Father Christmas or isn't there a Father Christmas? I wasn't sure, but there you are, he wasn't coming. Christmas morning there was a humming top, not from Father Christmas, but Mother Christmas. Because by that time farmer Jewitt had died, but his wife took over. She saw that my brother and I had something for Christmas.

Ernie Cheeseman

Trucks and an Engine

The people that lived next door, at Rowlands Gill, they had a laddy; he was the youngest of the family and he had everything you can imagine, they had money to buy him anything. But I didn't envy that laddy. We used to play with his toys and in the summer we used to take them into the backyard and sit and play with them. There were trucks and an engine set. And he had a rocking horse. Well, come Christmas he didn't need a lot really 'cos he had all sorts!

Joseph French

Donkey Boilers

I remember sneaking downstairs in the middle of the night. By the light of the fire I was able to see that my presents were on my side of the table occupied for meals and my brother's were on his side. We both had the same that Christmas – 'donkey boilers'. They were tiny little steam engines. You fitted a lamp full of methylated spirits and you filled the boiler with boiling water and when it got enough steam up it would drive a little wheel. And that's all, but it was magnificent. You got your face within an inch of it, watching, mesmerised. You wouldn't do it now, it's too dangerous.

Ernie Cheeseman

This lantern slide from around 1910 shows three children playing with a swing in a Stanley backyard.

A Dancing Peg Doll

We made a doll. The head was from an ordinary clothes peg, that's what we used, a clothes peg. When it comes to the split in the clothes peg, that was where the arms were, and wires through for the feet. There was two parts to the feet, a little bit and the clog. And you had a bit of string on the head. You sat on the edge of the cracket and somebody would whistle a tune, it would be, 'Oh Sally does tha like pease pudding, oh yes I do, la da da da dee di-dee, la da da da da dee dee', and so on.

Reece Eliot

Radio in the Bath

The tin bath used to be in the middle of the floor and dad would be sitting on a cracket getting washed like. He had like a crystal set, with earphones on, and he was listening to that the time he was bathing, and I knocked them off his head into the bath. Oooh, that was it! I don't think I sat down for a week after that. Because the men, the fathers, was boss in them days, boss of the family.

Derek Hall

A Stanley man listens to a valve radio.

A Cat's Whisker

The first wireless set I ever knew, John Gorland made it on the windowsill. A cat's whisker. And he had earphones, and he had it up to the tap in the pantry, a cold water tap. I was missing one day. They had me sat on a cracket with a matchbox on my head so the earphones would fit me. And I sat there goodness knows how long, until I was missed. Nobody knew where I was; they searched and couldn't find me. And there I was, sat in Gorland's pantry.

Ethel Murray

Buzzer Time

Our time signal was the buzzer at the pit, which of course was never Greenwich Mean Time, but it was certainly South Moor time, and that was how we went. Many years afterwards, when the wireless did come, in 1922 I think it would be, this chap bought himself a wireless, and at that time of course Big Ben would strike at twelve o'clock. It was a crystal set and of course he had earphones, cans as they called them then. 'Quiet everyone, listen, the clock's coming' – and there was Big Ben striking twelve o'clock. He brings out this whacking great watch and he looks at it and he says, 'You know, its a damn good clock they've got down in London, it hasn't lost not a minute since yesterday, I checked that, but I wonder why they keep it ten minutes fast?'!

Ernie Cheeseman

Three

BACKYARDS AND VILLAGE STREETS

Step Whitening

It was a competition to see who got their washing out first. We lived next door to a lady called Mrs Rutherford, and at five o'clock in the morning she would be out hanging the washing out. And she used to wash the front step every day, put new whitening on the front step, wash the pavement outside her house, wash her windows every single day. And you would see her with her sash windows open, sitting upstairs and leaning over the street washing her windows, with the sash windows pulled down over her knees to stop herself from falling out!

The whitening you got from the rag and bone man who came round. You'd give him the rags and bones and you would get the whitening. You thought you could tell what the state of a house was like inside by the washing or the state of the steps! You couldn't, but I used to hear people say, 'Look at her washing – what must her house be like? She doesn't whiten her step!' If you didn't whiten your step you really were a bit of a scruff weren't you?

John Williams and John Nicholson

Pig Keeping

Most miners kept a pig. If they didn't keep a pig they kept a goat, or poultry or rabbits, and they used to swap them round – there was no fridges in those days. When it was pig-killing day they used to share the pig out, so there was nothing wasted. And father used to go round, kill the pig for them.

Syd Wears

Locals gather around a newly killed pig in Crookhall.

Peelings for the Pig

They killed about a pig every year. It was a big day, the pig-killing day. All the neighbours got a part – you would go along the street, giving them a piece of the pig, spare ribs, black pudding, white pudding, sausage. And when they killed theirs, they returned it, you see. Everybody used to keep an old bath tin to keep the peelings in, potato and all sorts of vegetable peelings. And those that had pigs, they would go all over the village, calling, 'Do you have any peelings for the pig?' When they killed the pig, the people that had been giving peelings, they always gave them a little bit.

   They made black pudding with the blood; they would gash the throats and have the dish, stirring the blood all the time it was running out, to stop it from thickening. They used to put barley in, and lumps of fat, it was really good. Then the pig killer would come the next day and cut the pig up, and cover the bacon with saltpetre in order to cure it.

Jack Edgell

Coal Delivery

They delivered miner's concessionary coal on an open-backed lorry, which they would come and just tip outside your house. And my mother, along with lots of housewives, would have a little shovel with a short handle on and she would

A pair of children shovel coal up into a coal store on Joicey Square, Stanley.

shovel a load of coal into an open hatch. You'd take the hatch off from the back, put the boards up inside so the coals didn't spill in the yard, and shovel away.

John Nicholson

Middens

We had no hot water, just a cold water tap. And there was what they used to call the midden, the outdoor toilet in the yard. It was a big wood seat and the lid came up and you put your ashes and everything down there. Now then, the cart came around on Friday, and two men with shovels shovelled it all out! And they used to tip it in Andy Watts' field, and we used to play in the field, play with the boodies, collect the coloured glass and chop them up and make dolly mixtures, and make an oven with the clay, with bread and cakes to go in the oven — that's what we used to play with.

Doreen Scarrat

Toilet Paper

Toilet paper either wasn't available or wasn't invented. You tore off sheets of newspaper and you hung it on a nail which was on the back of the door on a bit of string or something like that. When the bin men used to come, they used to lift the steel hatch off the back of the thing. If it was a windy day when he used to bring his shovel out, all these bits of newspaper used to flutter down the street, all these soiled newspapers, and because we lived in a cul-de-sac they just used to flutter around. I used to be coming home from school and I knew then that the bin men had been that day because there were these soiled pieces of newspaper. Nobody collected them, they fluttered around and by the middle of the week they had gone.

John Nicholson

Annfield Plain Toilets

In Annfield Plain very few of the roads were tarmacadam, there were earthen roads in the majority of the area, and you had this toilet arrangement in the centre of the street. They were set up in blocks of four, two toilets at either end of the rectangular-type building. The rubbish or refuse from ashes would go into the centre part, and of course you had two toilets at each side for different families in the street. They were earth toilets. I never saw them because I was young at the time, but the night soil men would come and empty them out.

Jim Kay

A Proper War Dance

Seasonings that came then weren't as fine ground as they are now. They were lumpy and the salt was rock salt and you used to scrape a bit of salt off the rock and grind it with the flat of a knife. Pepper, nutmeg, mace and salt and pimento – it was rather lumpy so father used to put it onto newspaper and flatten it out with the flat of a broad knife. So father mixed the seasoning this day. He'd done this with the newspaper, just put it down, gone to serve a customer and the boss come running in, dying to go to the toilet. So he grabbed the paper and off he went. When he came back he was doing a proper war dance, saying, 'Oh my God my backside's on fire!'

Syd Wears

All the Mats Laid along the Hedge

There was a hedge right here and all the gardens went down to the railway. On a Friday morning, people would put their mats on this hedge that they were going to put down for the weekend. It used to get the sun you see. On the Friday night, the old mats was bundled away in a cupboard, and the good ones went down for the weekend. Then, on Monday morning, up those good mats came and folded away again.

Jack Edgell

Making Ice Cream

In the backyard they used to have a boiler with a pan of milk, and they used to make the mix for the ice cream. They put the milk in, corn flour, and they used to boil it up. They used to have to freeze it by hand, put the mix into a can – it was surrounded by ice on the outer drum – then they used to have to turn it round and round with a wooden handle. It froze on the outside of the can and they used to have to scrape it off the side of the can with a stick, and turn it again. Gradually, what used to be a sort of a milk used to thicken up and eventually came into a sort of an ice cream and the more they turned it the smoother it got. It was a lot of hard work!

Joseph Dragone

The Communal Ovens

The communal ovens would be on every week. The women used to get the timber at the pit – old pit timbers – and put them in the oven. They used to get it red hot, and after it all burnt out it was all red. They used to have a long shovel to put the bread to the back. Everybody used to mark their tins, which was theirs. After the bread was out I think they used to push the teacakes in, see, the oven would just be right. These ovens were smashing for making lovely teacakes.

Jack Edgell

The Steamroller

In 1922, just before I started school, they were repairing the road in front of our house and the steamroller was going and of course that was like a bee to a honeypot to me. The roller man would have a little hut and if he was too far from home he would live in it, but he was too close to Stanley so he took his roller back home and I followed it. Mother knew my weakness for everything mechanical and she said, 'I bet he has gone after the roller!' She caught me just before we went under Tommy's Arch, at the top of Tommy's Lane, which is now Park Road off South Moor.

Ernie Cheeseman

Women of High Row, South Moor, feeding their free-range chickens, *c.* 1900. The street was demolished in 1916.

Window cleaners from Stanley Window Cleaning Company.

The Streets of Beamish

The streets were dirt – just an earth road. We had a footpath at the front, and the road at the front was like little stones, through the years they had gone smooth. At the back was a dirt road, and they were swept clean as well. There was no tarmac roads then, on the colliery rows. We never took any harm as kids playing in the dirt. We used to go to the Hell's Hole Road and play. There was a stream in that road, we played there, and the farmer would let us play in the corner of his field.

Ethel Murray

Horse Traffic

Co-operative carts came, the grocery came, the butcher came, the coal horse and cart came, the midden man came with his horse and cart, so you would get quite a bit of traffic and you would get a rut or two which would of course get all 'clarty', as we used to say. So it needed filling in. Well, if you filled it in with ashes it was great when it was wet, but in the dry summers we seem to have had then it got dusty. So we used to fill the ruts with coal. I wonder if it's still there?

Ernie Cheeseman

Car Repair

In the 1940s my dad had a really old veteran car. Even when I was a kid it was very old. It was always breaking down; we had to do all the repairs ourselves. When it was pouring down and you were underneath the car it was just dripping down as it was a four-sided gutter. We got to lie on the cobbles – so we got the clippy mat out the hall and laid it on the cobbles and because of its thickness and the joints in the cobbles the rain on the road ran through the joints and under the clippy mat, so were kept quite dry for something like half the length of the job, and then we got another clippy mat!

Les Stringer

Washing Lines

Every house had two, possibly three lines of washing out. And of course if it was raining you would have to get it all in because if the rain came down in a dust-laden atmosphere that's all your work undone. Wash day moved from Wednesday to Monday. I think it was because there was no coal carts coming along on Monday.

Ernie Cheeseman

Ice-Cream Seller

When grandfather was in Gateshead, he used to have the handcart and he used to push up Marley Hill, Greenside, all these high-up places, and he used to push this barrow all the way up. Must have took some doing like, because the trouble with ice cream was it was surrounded by salt and ice and it was really heavy, you know. It took a lot of pushing like to get up to Sunniside, Marley Hill. So it was a long, hard day. I remember going up there with a horse and cart with him. I was only a young lad then, I used to fall asleep in the back of the cart.

Joseph Dragone

Street Sellers

There was a man who came round selling oil, and the knife grinder, and a muffin man came round. He had a cart. And the milkman came; he had a churn, you see, with a scoop. Fishwives came from North Shields with the creels and the blue uniforms. And a woman – we called her the pot woman – she came from South Shields I think. She would carry a clothes basket. You gave her clothes and

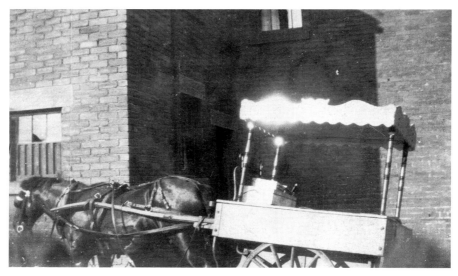

Johnson's ice-cream van, photographed here in Beamish village.

she would give you pottery; Maling ware for instance. And of course there were tramps. They used to come round regularly as well, wanting a drink of water or a piece of bread or something.

Dora Black

Fishwives

There used to be a fishwife who came on a train to Beamish station. She was a stooped old woman; she use to carry two bags of fish and she would drop one bag of fish on the pavement and head to the Shepherd and Shepherdess. Around Chophill Colliery there were a lot of streets and she would sell those fish round there and then come back and pick her other fish up, which no one ever touched, and then walk down towards Beamish Club area and sell them down there.

John Nicholson

A Postgirl in World War One

We started around seven o'clock – it all depended on how long it took us to sort our own mail up. You see, each of us got our own delivery and we had to sort them into streets ourselves, there was no machine. We had hobnailed boots fastened up with laces, with heel plates and toe plates. Our uniforms at the bottom was all leather-bound to stop it from wearing so soon. And a dark navy blue, like the fishermen's – you never got wet through. We used to get measured for them

This travelling salesman of draperies was raising funds for New Kyo Wesleyan Mission.

Cullercoats fishwife Mrs Taylor. It is recorded that she bought the first ticket to Annfield Plain when the new line was opened in February 1894.

Eliza Brown (*née* Jameson) worked at Stanley Post Office during the First World War. This photograph, showing her postgirl's uniform, was taken in 1918, when she was twenty years old.

twice a year and our boots twice a year, and mind we went through them. I'd go home with my shoulders bleeding, you know, because the mailbags were heavy, especially at Christmas time.

Eliza Brown

Delivering Telegrams

The post office used to get all the telegrams to deliver. This lad was always hanging around the post office, to do the telegrams. He'd left school – probably fifteen. He used to have an armband on and he got one and three for going to Hedley Hall with that telegram. Short distances, he probably got threepence or tuppence. I used to go with him for a walk, you see.

Jack Edgell

Post in the Snow

Sometimes the police used to escort me because it was quite dark in the winter time and we had snowstorms where you couldn't get into some of the houses. One day I was going up behind the snow plough – that was the only way I could get along to East Stanley – and I went to the post office. A policeman was standing there and he was waving me not to go any further. I had a whole lot of letters for East Street, and I was walking up the bank. But there was no bank, the snow was so thick it was at the top of the houses and when I got so far up I found a chimney stack. The policeman came flying up and he said, 'Come on, you can't do any more.' Three days they didn't get any letters; they couldn't get anything to eat.

Eliza Brown

Calling the Kids In

Another feature of life at the time was when the mothers used to come out and get the kids in at night time. They would stand at the door or walk to the bottom of the street and shout out their first name, these women screeching each kid's name, 'GEORDIE!' We could be miles away.

John Nicholson

This group of children were photographed for the *Durham Advertiser* in August 1935. One group are having a tea party in this Stanley backstreet, while another boy plays with a toy car.

Skipping Rope

Well, skipping was one of the things, you know; skip by yourself, or two people held each end of the rope and you skipped in the rope. And we used to play another game called monty kitty. Somebody stood against the house wall, you know, bent like that, and then your friends all took turns in jumping on your back, you know, and not just one at a time!

Margaret Hall

Marbles in the Gutter

I can recall playing marbles all the way back from (West Pelton) school – half in the gutter and half in the road. There wasn't the traffic.

John Nicholson

Each Season had its Game

Each season used to have its game. There would be marbles, and just about spring time when the days were getting longer, we used to come down here with hoops. The boys used to have iron ones, but the girls used to have wooden ones. Before going to school, we'd come down the road – there was very little traffic then and it was horse traffic – and so many weeks would be hoops and so many weeks it would be marbles and then there'd be skipping ropes. And then there'd be bays – we used to mark it out with chalk. And then there'd be ball games, and at the beginning of the winter time we'd play 'kick the block', you know, we'd have a block and a ring, somebody would kick it away and then somebody would have to go and seek it and then the other ones would go away and hide.

R. Powton

Pranks

I don't think we ever had a name for this, but what we used to do, especially if we got some matches – we'd get some paper, and you know the down-comer on a house, the rain drops off a roof into a gulley and then there is a down-comer down to the bottom. Well it comes to an angle with a foot like that. You stuff that very, very loosely with paper, as much as you can, with a piece sticking out, and then you light the paper and then of course once you got the natural draught there was an awful noise. People in the houses could hear it. 'What are you doing?' We would run away!

Ernie Cheeseman

Children throw snowballs outside Annfield Plain Co-op drapery department.

Alley Football

We used to play football in the morning, then go and get your dinner and come back again and then join another side. There was maybe twenty or thirty blokes playing and sometimes the lasses would play, that just would go on all day.

At No Place, there was an area at the other end of the street, and we used to play a game of doors. You would select one door at either side of the street as a goal. You would dribble in the street and then kick, I mean really bang against somebody's back door. I can't recollect a lot of people objecting but they must have done – twenty goals banging off somebody's back door. And if the ball went over somebody's backyard you would go next door and go over the wall and come back.

Eddie and John Nicholson

The Gangway

We were playing football or cricket. Sods law would decree that every other ball would go over on the gangway as we called it – and we would look, check ourselves, and run across and pick the ball up and come back again. No one was ever hurt. Can you imagine that today? They would be killing kids every other day wouldn't they?

Ernie Cheeseman

Stone Throwing

You wore short trousers until you were twelve, thirteen or fourteen. You would gan somewhere and fill your pockets full of stones so the pockets would hang below the trousers, full of stones, and you would go and have stone fights! Almost all the lads – because your haircut then was shaved well up – the hair never used to grow because they had been hit on the back of the head with stones! So we used to face each other, Grange Villa or somewhere, and throw stones at each other until we were fed up, then we put down the stones and went home.

John Nicholson

Pan Shovel Slides

Hustledown wasn't only a tip for the spoil heap for the colliery, it was also a tip for domestic waste. Believe me there was stuff that antique dealers would give their right eye for. There was this wonderful Aladdin's cave, albeit rather mucky.

Four Stanley footballers – possibly a father and his sons, *c.* 1920.

Annfield Plain Park, complete with lake and bandstand. In the background can be seen the station footbridge.

At that time ninety per cent of South Moor had dry toilets and that went on the tip as well. You can understand why we had diphtheria and what have you! But to us lads it was a magnificent place to hunt and see if we could find anything. And of course we would come across a pan shovel, clamber up the top, and we would skate down – wonderful, absolutely wonderful.

Ernie Cheeseman

South Moor Park

We used to play in the back street. We would play football, cricket, rounders, hot rice, marbles, tab pictures – we used to throw a tab picture down, and then throw, and if you cover that one, you kept it. We spent a lot of time in South Moor Park as kiddies, you know, nowhere else to go to like. There was a paddling pool there and swings. But when the park keeper come around to lock that park you had to get out, no cheek. You got out like!

Derek Hall

'Tarry Tooters'

The ropes [on the endless ropeway] wore out and had to be changed quite regularly. The Holmside and South Moor Coal company used to sell them to farmers for hedge rope. And of course they would weather off and rust now that there was no oil on them and we lads used to like to get the rope in the centre and light it. It used to smoulder like anything in the dark. In those days there was only gas lights and they were very far between, so South Moor outside at that time was a very dark place. If you got into a really dark place where you couldn't see anything at all except this glowing thing, we would make all sorts of pictures by swinging them round. Other lads would say, 'Oh I can make a better figure of eight,' that sort of thing. We called them 'tarry tooters'. We used to say, 'Have you got a bit of tarry toot?' When we got home we used to get a hiding off mam, 'You've been tarry tooting again! Where did you get the matches?'

Ernie Cheeseman

Coke Ovens

The coke ovens were like large Eskimo igloos but built in firebrick – it was where they used to put the coal and gradually fire it off to coke, you see. These were no longer used at all but they made lovely houses. We could not have had a better adventure playground. It was magnificent even for girls and certainly for boys, with all these engines puffing away.

Ernie Cheeseman

Four

DOWN THE SHOPS

Getting a Co-op Job

I went to the Co-op in 1942, that was when the men were all getting called up and they were advertising for married women. Well I'd been married about a year, maybe. In those days you couldn't get pinnies and that, your mams made them out of sugar bags, a hessian apron. This Monday, I had this hessian apron on and I was helping my mam to wash. My mam was saying to me, 'Ella get that apron off!' I thought she was gone mad – what in the world what did she want the apron for? Anyhow, Mr Carr, the general manager, had pulled up at the back gate. He had a chauffeur, them days, Billy Morden. And he came up to the back door, knocked at the door. I went down the steps and he says, 'Mrs Smith, I've got a job for you in the grocery, could you start at one o'clock today?' I says, 'Yes, I can, but I've got no overall.' 'No trouble, go to the grocery department, ask for Mr Fenwick, and he'll take you to the millinery and they'll fix you up with overalls.' And I was there right up till the old Co-op closed.

Rachel Smith

Annfield Plain Co-op

All the shops were together in a row right down the front street of Annfield Plain. The Co-op took the whole length of the street starting from the carpets, menswear, hardware, grocery, butchers, chemists, cake shop, greengrocery, jewellers, all the way down. In the grocery department we had the odd little bars of chocolate on the counter – tuppenny bars, penny bars – to buy the kids while the mums were waiting to be served in the shop. In those days once you'd been in the back shop for a while, you could be allowed to serve in the shop. You learned all the prices by heart and you had to absorb them.

Ronald Ledger

Butchers thought to be at Annfield Plain Co-op.

Vermin in the Co-op

Mice, of course, could get behind fixtures; it wasn't uncommon to open a drawer and find mice scurrying around. There was very little you could do about it, it's difficult to get an animal that small from behind wooden areas. They would be in the yard where you have grain, horses, and in actual fact I have seen a rat just drop onto a horse's back, the horse didn't move but I did!

The bacon came in sacks and would be hung up in the cellar. Now during the winter it wasn't so bad, but during the summer it was absolutely horrendous, I have never seen anything like it actually, it was difficult to keep flies off it. It was wrapped in muslin, of course, but you were forever having to scrape it down and dry it and try and make it as presentable as possible. When the flies were in, there were maggots. You wouldn't dispense with it because you had a few maggots there, but that would have to be cleaned out.

Jim Kay

Paper Packaging

Most of the tea was pre-packed, quarter pounds. We used to grind our own coffee; we had a little coffee grinder on the counter and a container of coffee beans. It was very popular, ground coffee. For that, you'd make a little bag, twist the bag and twist the bottom, pour a quarter pound of coffee in, and you made your own little packets from squares of paper.

They made the cones for anything of that nature: yeast, that was done the same way, and all your little range of drawers in behind the counters, all your little spices, cinnamon, mixed spice, ground ginger and that, they were weighed up much the same, except they were weighed by ounces.

Ronald Ledger

The Grocery Department

There were three counters for groceries, one bill counter and one long provision counter, marble topped, a long brass fitting along the top for hanging the meat, a hand-operated bacon machine. There was an Avery scale, a cheeseboard, half-moon cheese knife, an area where you'd serve, and then another area where you would cut these large barrels of butter. The Co-op usually dealt in Danish butter, it was beautiful butter that. That would be the job of the youngsters to knock the hoops off the barrels, beech wood casks, remove the paper from the butter. Behind there was another marble slab where you would put up the provisions for the grocery orders. Then you would have the tube for the Lamson Cash retrieval system. Then another small slicing machine for cooked meats – of course during the war there were very few cooked meats available so that machine more or less just stood.

Jim Kay

This picture of a grocer's shop interior comes from a series of magic lantern slides.

Making up the Orders

All your dried fruit came in cases or boxes and that was all weighed up in the back shop. When I first started we used squares of paper, and then that was folded over and then the ends tucked in. Then you had bags for rice, for all your dried pulses, peas, lentils and all that, they were all weighed in the back shop from bulk sacks.

Ronald Ledger

Temptations

Lizzie Tulip was the cleaner. Her sister was a good cook and she used to cook these little teacakes and she used to bring them back to the shop. The two men, Mr Buglass and Mr Brown, they used to slice the butter, you know, and they used to put it on the teacakes – ee God, it was lovely. And that was wor ten o'clocks. Why there was some good biscuits, and I went up to about thirteen stone. It was a wonder Bill knew me when he come back from leave …

Rachel Smith

Weighing up the Flour

In 1939 I was employed by the Co-op in what was termed the flour warehouse. There was myself and two older men worked in there and it was a full-time job in those days, weighing the flour. There was all the feeding stuff for the hens, and pigeon corn as well, we even sold dog biscuits, and you supplied the travelling shops too. The flour in those days all came down chutes into the hopper. It came in every Thursday, four or five loads in the course of the day. Quite often whoever was weighing the flour got deluged with flour if we forgot to close the trapdoor when it was being filled up, and he'd finish up looking like a snowman. The sacks of flour were ten stones. All the flour was ten stones, most of the other stuff was eight-stone bags, so you had a bit of humping to do, 'cos you get an awful lot of flour in the course of a week.

Ronald Ledger

Bought Bread

There was bought bread to be had from Kelly's at South Moor and Kelly's at Stanley. It was baked by Hunter's in a big bakery at Gateshead. In fact there was a ditty:

Bakers staff from West Stanley Co-op outside the premises on Front Street, Stanley.

Hunter's bread tastes like lead.
Take one bite and drop down dead.
Follow the swallow back home.

That's what we thought of bought bread – horrible!

Ernie Cheeseman

Tuppenny Cream Cakes

The customers for bread and tuppenny cream cakes were either people who had businesses of some sort or were officials – they could afford it. It was convenient occasionally for a widow but generally the people who were a little bit better off bought the bread and they bought the tuppenny cream cakes and they bought the peach melbas, the big cakes – they used to be about one shilling and thrupence.

Vincent Morris

Christmas Biscuits

The majority of people seemed to make their own Christmas puddings, although we would stock some of course. But dried fruits, flour, ginger wine essence – the Co-op made their own. We did a limited amount of confectionery specially for Christmas time, but the biggest ones was the biscuits. They used to make a big display in the centre of the floor with all the tinned biscuits, shortbreads, and hope that would bring business. In later years all that expanded; you'd start selling Christmas cards, selection boxes, Christmas crackers.

Ronald Ledger

The Week Before Christmas

There would be later opening hours the last week in Christmas, to get all the deliveries done. It was a good job going out for grocery orders. We had a long book all printed with the various things – butter, lard, marg, tea, sugar, soaps, biscuits, jams – and we would get this book on Monday, Tuesday, and Wednesday perhaps as well, go round peoples houses and get the grocery orders, and over the next two days they were assembled and delivered with the horse and cart, or the lorry for the far places. At Christmas time it was difficult to get round because everybody insisted you had a glass of sherry or port or a whiskey, and it was a well-known fact that the butcher carts in particular drank so much that the horse found its own way home.

Tom Tate

The Cigarette Kiosk

Mr Bramley was manager of the grocery and he said, 'Ella, would you like to go in the kiosk?' It was just cigarettes and tobacco, and it was by the door. I used to keep the door open a bit, so I was getting a bit of air. He came once or twice and shut it – anybody could have hit on us for the little bit of money that was there, and the cigarettes. All six of us went around together and everyone one of them smoked, and I could have been sick, the smell of the tobacco!

Rachel Smith

Chewing Tobacco

Tobacco was another thing which we weighed, especially the chewing tobacco. You had to weigh it, cut off the ounce. The miners took a lot of the chewing tobacco with them into the pits because they weren't allowed to smoke, of course, but they could chew. We had some which was in a big flat coil. It was called 'target'; it was about an inch and a half broad and three quarters of an inch deep and you cut it off in little blocks. That was a pipe tobacco and people used to have their little sharp knives and cut away at it, you know, for their pipes.

Ronald Ledger

Taken in around 1914 on Front Street, Stanley, this photograph shows Jenny Morecroft leading the horse and cart of Morecroft's milk round, which delivered around the Stanley district.

Gunpowder

There was no gunpowder magazine in the pit. At South Moor, they used to buy their powder at the local shops – hardware shops – and this chap used to get boxes to put his powder in and he was putting his powder into the tin in front of the fire one morning and a spark flew out – it lifted the roof top!

Robert Gardiner

Working in the Chemist

The smells were lovely, perfumes and soaps, and then there was the testers, you know, you could have a little dip! Mr Liddle did all the prescriptions. On a Saturday morning we used to get a lot of young men in and I used to wonder why they stood back when you went to say, 'Can I help you?' They didn't want you serving them! I was as green as grass, I must have been – it was years after I realised why they wanted Mr Liddle, they didn't want us!

Rachel Smith

A Corner Shop

Shop hours didn't mean a lot to everybody, because if the shop was closed they would come and rattle the sneck at the back door – disturb you whatever you were doing to buy something from the shop. A lot of people would do that. The shop sold general household things, sweets, chocolate, flour, bread, general household things, polishes, sanitary towels, cigarettes, Carters little liver pills and Beecham's powders, lemon glycerine and honey cough mixtures …

John Nicholson and John Williams

Everything so Delicious

There was a stone house that was the post office. Everybody used to go to the post office and have a good old gossip. Next to the post office there was a general dealers called Drapers. Next to Drapers was the Miss Lumleys and they were bakers. They used to bake lovely cakes and custard tarts and pies, everything so delicious, ham and egg pies. In fact, when we lived at Twisel, and my mother was having special visitors, I used to go through the woods to the Lumleys' bakery to buy the pies or tarts. And next to that used to be a tobacconist and stationers – it was very high class; they sold the very best of everything.

Irene Wilson

This greengrocer's shop was photographed in 1935 for the *Durham Advertiser.*

Quaking Houses Shops

The house across here used to be a general dealer. My mother used to gan there for nearly all our stuff. It was, 'Mr Pennington, can my mam have a loaf of bread?' 'Why aye!' He had a big book, used to mark it down, and maybe on a Friday, when your dad got his wages, you might be able to pay something off it, you might not.

There was a Co-operative, you got the dividend there – my mother's check number was 6570, I can always remember that – and we used to get a bit dividend off it like. Thirlaway's shop used to stand up in that corner, it was a good shop, that; she used to take jam jars in, she would give you a penny for a jam jar.

Derek Hall

Rate Collecting for Dad

It was my ambition to be a telephonist. To be a telephonist in them days you had to get a recommendation from a postmaster or postmistress. I saw myself getting dressed up and going by train every morning to Newcastle. I tried for the job and I got it, but my father wouldn't let me accept – he said I was more use to him at home. I was good at maths and things, so with him being a rate collector I used to go out and seek the rates. He always warned me, only put sovereigns and half sovereigns in the bag, and keep the sovereigns away from the copper and the silver. I used to go and bank the money for my father at Martins Bank at Annfield Plain. People knew I was taking money to the bank but nobody approached you. Mr Barrow was the bank manager, he knew my father and I was allowed to go and bank the money, do everything.

Mrs Linsley

Five

LEISURE TIME

Dance Halls and Reading Rooms

An awful lot of dancing used to go on, for instance, Stanley had the Co-op, upstairs there's a lovely dance floor. There was a Saturday night hop there. There was the Pallida Dance which was at the bottom of Front Street, Stanley – that was very, very popular. At the top of Shield Row Bank, just round the corner from the Royal Hotel, at the bottom on the right-hand side, is the Hibernian; lovely dance floor. There was the St Andrew's Church Institute, there was a lovely dance floor and there was an awful lot of dancing there. Along at Catchgate they not only had dancing, they had roller-skating.

There were still reading rooms open, I can barely remember the reading room open above the Co-op at South Moor. I can certainly remember the reading room above the Co-op building at Stanley. There was also a reading room and library along at Catchgate.

Ernie Cheeseman

Firewatching and Dancing

We used to have to fire watch, take our turn. You got, I think, two shilling; you did it about once a month. And of course they used to give it to the young ones and the young ones used to go off to the dance at Castles. And some of the army lads were stationed in the store yard, where they used to have the cooker, and they used to make supper. The young ones thought it was ideal, they had the two shilling, they went to the dance, they come back, they got fed. I lived at South Moor and I didn't get home, I used to go to my friend's house for my breakfast. I hated it, 'cos I used to imagine mice and all sorts – 'cos it was the billiard hall, a great big hall, and you were just on like a little bunk thing.

Rachel Smith

This dance band had their photograph taken professionally in Arcade Square, Chester-le-Street, in January 1934.

Meeting Girls at the Dance

These dances, there was no alcohol; you couldn't buy alcohol, not like the way they are now. It was a cup of tea, or a bottle of pop. So we used to have a few pints in the pub then up the dance floor at quarter past nine, pay our half a crown in. Used to finish at eleven o'clock. A proper dance band on. I think a lot of lads would meet their wives at these dances. You just got on talking to them, take them home, maybes have a few more dates. You had the Pally at the bottom of the street – on a Friday night that was – from six to seven was like a junior dance. On Tuesday night it was Teddy Boy night. That used to finish at eleven as well. Then there was the Co-op on a Saturday night. That's where I met Joan, at a Co-operative dance at Stanley. There was Castles at Annfield Plain, that was on a Friday night, ten o'clock until two in the morning. Many a time I've gone there and I've been sitting asleep. Someone would give me a nudge, 'Eh, the dance has finished!'

Derek Hall

Tin Hall

I remember when Rowlands Gill first had a picture hall and a dance hall, it was built for roller skates then they started to use it for roller skating and dancing.

It lasted for quite a while, it was only corrugated sheeting, and the picture hall was the same. Sometimes the lights went out and you had to gan and get a ticket to go again the next night! It was joined together, all wood and corrugated sheeting.

Joseph French

Co-op Staff Leisure

Above most Co-operative buildings you would find areas for leisure pursuits. At Annfield Plain, there was a billiard room, a reading room, function room. Now usually the function room was used for weddings, receptions, meetings of that type. On Friday night there was usually a meeting for the staff, we had a table tennis table, we did have the occasional Beetle Drive, Whist Drive, maybe a little dance now and again, someone was always there able to play the piano, of course. We had some good nights there.

Jim Kay

Sheet Cinema

These two brothers bought round a cinematograph, like the pictures, and some films. They had a big hut in the garden so of course it come out like, 'He's gonna show'.

In December 1937 the *Durham Advertiser* captured this photo of children queuing outside the Essoldo Cinema, Stanley, to watch *The Cave-In.*

And he had this white sheet and put it at the front, and of course they made little seats. And we sat down, and it was pins to get in – you took pins to get in. And he showed you a good show. Of course the films weren't elaborate like they are now, you know, but there was something worth a see. Then of course he'd be there the next day and you'd see something else.

Joseph French

Saturday Matinee

On a Saturday afternoon, Tom Mix and his horse Tony were on at the Arcadia, the Saturday afternoon matinee. It was a penny to get in. And if we were late in getting in there, the man on the door who took you pennies off you was no longer there and they hadn't locked the door so you would get in for nowt!

We never came straight home after the matinee – because the streets of South Moor became the plains of cowboy land and we were cowboys and what have you. South Moor was mid-West America. And we eventually got home to a tea which very often on a Saturday would be toasted muffins, because you would get the muffin man coming around on a Saturday afternoon.

Ernie Cheeseman

Ice-Cream Cafe

We all worked in the shop when we came home from school. We served, made coffee and tea, Oxo. I mean with living up above the shop, if they got busy well you came downstairs, you did your homework and then you had to go into the shop. There was no off at the weekends; Saturday and Sundays we were all in the shop. People just used to come in, have a cup of tea, an ice cream, sandwich, a cup of coffee, talk.

Raffaelo Moscardini

Pit Electricity

In 1923, Stanley was virtually without electrical power. Now that isn't completely true because the William pit supplied electricity to the Wesleyan Chapel and the Primitive Methodist Chapel. But you see there were also other places that required electricity like the Arcadia Cinema at South Moor, the Tivoli, and there was three at Stanley. So there's five cinemas which required electricity for their projectors. They also supplied electricity to their next-door neighbours at South Moor – the South Moor Hotel, which was next to the Arcadia, and also the

Members of the Crook-Stanley Community Centre physical training group, photographed for the *Northern Echo*.

Meadow Dairy and Loweries, the wool shop. They were supplied with electricity but only while the pictures were showing.

Ernie Cheeseman

A Pound

A pound was a good pocket money then. You could do anything with a pound – gan to the pictures every night, take a girlfriend to the pictures, maybe have a couple of drinks. But then you didn't take girls into the pubs, not like the way it is now. If you took a girl into a pub men used to look and say, 'I bet she's a queer 'un, she's in the pub.' So you just used to gan to the pictures.

Derek Hall

Pub Work at Thirteen

My father was a publican till he went into the First World War. When he went, my grandmother had the Durham Ox, and I had to take charge. I was just thirteen years old, so we had to get a special license for me to serve in the pub. My aunt

A group gather at Hammer Square, Beamish, for 'a merry party'. The musicians include Mr Laverick on the mouth organ, Mr Craggs on the melodian and Mr Corker playing fiddle.

was a cripple so she used to serve in the bar, and I did all the cellar work and then wait on as well, at thirteen.

Jack Edgell

Pub Fights

Them publics were nearly always full at weekends – Saturdays and Sundays. They were crowded because the beer was that cheap, you see, and when they got a lot of this strong beer, there used to be a lot of fighting going on in the Hilltop. Every Sunday night you would see people of all ages waiting to see which public opened the door – one would open and some men would come out and fight. These were open-air boxing bouts, they used to fight like tigers and it was just the beer making them fight. And they used to knock each others' teeth out and they used to break their glasses and all sorts. They would work with each other next morning.

Samuel Jackson

A South Moor boxer poses
for the camera.

A Fine Summer's Night

In the 1926 strike there was no halls or anything open for people to go and have
a dance, so they put somebody's piano and somebody had a fiddle and somebody
had something else, onto a cart, took it to the schoolyard, and that's where they
had a dance, in the open, on a fine summer's night.

Ethel Murray

Sangsters Circus

They used to have the circuses on the green there. That was a marvellous time for
young 'uns. They always came in by road. They had everything in those days, there
were elephants and tigers. They would come down Front Street, with the drums

banging, trumpets playing, and the clowns dancing and all that. We used to follow them down, come dancing in with them. There were sideshows and there were only carbide lamps and paraffin flares. I always remember that the bloke who used to draw the crowds, he had a peg leg. They used to build this great big tower, sixty or seventy feet up, and he had this little tank of water, about four foot at the most. And he used to dive off. Pour paraffin on himself, set light to his clothes and then dive off! It was a marvellous sight to see. And there was strong men, they would bend these great big iron bars. One of them used to lie on the deck and they used to put a slab of stone on his chest – maybe half a hundredweight – then he would invite you to hit him with a sledgehammer. Aye we would just take it in turns with this sledge hammer whacking this bloody great stone until it broke. You had like a big tent in the middle which was like a big circus tent. All the cages were all the way round. You used to have two big bears wrestling and kangaroos boxing, it was bloody marvellous.

Anonymous

Races

Down here on the cricket field you've got South Moor Club, which was called Mickeys, and the S Club. They used to have a sports day on, and the two clubs would hurl down the cricket field. There were whippet races, and quoits. And a beer tent there, and the bookmakers. One lad used to live up here, Robert Roxburgh – we used to call him Robby – he used to gan to grammar school and

Members of the Annfield Plain Boys Brigade begin a race in August 1935. (*Durham Advertiser*)

The keeper saves a goal during a match between Stanley United and Bishop Auckland, February 1948. (*Durham Advertiser*)

he represented England at running. He ran the 100 yards and he was breaking that tape five or six yards before anybody else. And his uncle had £25 on him in the last race. But what they did, they handicapped him. Put him back four yards and he just got beat. If someone had only gone to him and said, 'Son, divven't win by five yards, just win by one,' then he wouldn't have been handicapped in the final.

Derek Hall

Shrove Tuesday Football

On Shrove Tuesday every shop from top to bottom of Front Street in Chester-le-Street boarded its windows up. You couldn't walk up the street because of the crowds. They used to come in from all over the county. They used to throw the ball out about ten o'clock in the morning, and chase that ball wherever it went. And of course the Burn was open then, the ball used to go in there. Everybody was in, men and women, especially the younger women like, you know. As you went up to Pelton you would go across the fields kicking the ball and the crowds would be following you and then back into Newfield and then Pelton Fell – wherever the ball went you just followed it, it was kicked around and around. It had to be back at that same pub and whoever had the ball when they went into that pub got a firkin of beer, which is about nine gallons or something. And there was a lad called Pickles and he always turned out in a football strip. He would go home and have his dinner and all sorts and then come out and chase it again and join in but at the end of that day he would invariably have that blinking ball.

Anonymous

Sunday Football

On a Sunday, we would get across the fell. There used to be a football field there, half a crown a man. It would be about twenty on each side, with their pit boots on and everything. When Quaking Houses had a team, the players used to strip in different people's houses, the goalkeeper stripped in this one with my brother-in-law (he played for them as well) and other players stripped in different houses 'cos they hadn't a stripping hut at the time.

Derek Hall

Black Backs

Are you aware of the fact that a huge section of miners never washed their backs? I remember going on a pitman's family outing. The teenagers, they were going to have a swim in the sea, so they stripped off on the beach, they were in their costumes which came down to just below their knees. And of course miners in the winter time or if they were on the dayshift never saw the sun from one weekend to another. So they were deathly white with an absolutely black back. It always sticks in my mind that. The chalk-white face and the chalk-white hands, and the back was absolutely black.

Ernie Cheeseman

Yew Tops Band

There used to be a colliery band play at Yew Tops. There were lots of colliery bands in those days; Handenhold and places like that had their own bands. They had uniforms, sort of a navy jacket and trousers with a gold bit of braid on and a cap. They had a cloth on the ground for you to throw in whatever you could afford, ha'pennies and pennies in those days. And if you were walking along what we called 'the bottom' you could hear them quite clearly.

Iris Summers

Sunday Evening Walks

There was up Sandy Lonnen a well-worn path to the Shield Row Drift Mine. It was plantation actually. There was lovely walks there, every conceivable type of wildflower was there. Those days the paths were well cleared.

Ernie Cheeseman

A Day at the Forges

Beamish had a station in them days, and poor children would come from Gateshead for a day to play down the Forges. Mr Bob Oliphant and his wife used to have a stall, and make tea for them down the flat field in the forges where the waterfall is, and we were asked at school to take our balls and skippy ropes down, and make ourselves friendly and play with these children. When they whistled to take them up to Beamish station we'd go up and put our arms around them and be friendly with them, and I think when that train went away there wasn't a dry eye amongst them or us.

Ethel Short

Games in the Park

We used to go from East Stanley to the park. There was a flat piece on the top and we used to do racing. I was pretty good at it at the time, I won a prize. Then of course we always had a bag of cakes, you know, they used to supply us with a bag of cakes. The members used to make them up and then sort them out and everybody got a cake or two.

Anonymous

Field Day, 1926

Mr Oxley, who farmed the Stanley Burn Farm, he was a member of the chapel and he used to let the field off to them, free of charge of course, to have a field day, as we used to call it. It was an ordinary meadow but he would keep his cows off it probably for a month beforehand so that any cowpats would be dried out nicely. There were three-legged races, sack races, egg and spoon races and all that sort of thing. Of course the farmhouse would supply the hot water to make the tea. There was no marquee; it was all out in the open. Thank goodness it was a lovely summer that 1926 summer and each of we children got a bag of goodies – a meat pie, a salmon sandwich and two cream cakes.

Ernie Cheeseman

Pitch and Toss

The men used to get two pennies on the fingers, like that, hie them up a height, and spin them, and bet on if it was two heads. When it was up you'd say two heads, or two tails. Some used to use a two-headed penny, a head on each side, so you couldn't lose. Pitch and toss was illegal – you had to watch for the police. It used to be terrible across the Grange and Pelton Fell for pitch and toss.

Mr Huscroft

Pich and Toss Pennies

Pitch and toss, my dad was pretty lucky at that. He used to have two pennies, he used to rub them, get them bright, practically rub the head off, you know. Well in these houses there was a penny meter, you used to put a penny in to get your light on. Well of course our light went out, and my mother went into my father's waistcoat, got these two pennies out, put them in the machine, put the light on. On the Sunday when he put his waistcoat on, he put his hand in – gone. Mother had to tell him where she put them; he had a good idea himself. He went and he pulled the bottom of the meter off, all the pennies was there, he got his two out.

Being kids we used to lie up on the quarry tops, watching for the police coming. I remember once the police come, and we shouted down to the men. The police turned around and says, 'Jack, you needn't run, your name's top of the list.' He was reeling other ones off, telling them not to run because their names was already down.

Derek Hall

Pinky Bowry

I've seen them place half a dollar a time – that was big money in them days – on what they called pinky bowry. Did you ever see the little pinkers? You don't see them now – about two inches diameter, and a metal ring a yard in circumference. Each man had to put a marble in there. The man on first had no chance. The next man naturally would try and knock a marble out. If he knocked one out he's on this fellow, if he was hit he had to forego half a crown. Great big fellas played this, coal hewers. Where we lived was a cul-de-sac and I've seen them down the back there, at the end of the bay.

Reece Eliot

Quoit Making

With the rope haulage system, you obviously had these little pulleys to get them round the corner and direct the rope where you wanted them. These little pulleys would be about ten inches diameter and the groove right around them would be

A quoits game near South Moor.

very, very deep and of course with the rope in them they would wear out and the ring would drop off eventually – lovely for quoits.

Ernie Cheeseman

Quoits

There was quoits all the time up here. My dad, he was a good player. And there was a man called Harry Rostron, he was the world champion. My dad used to say that man could take his gold watch off his waistcoat, thirty foot away, put it on the ground, throw a quoit and ring it. He says, 'I've even seen him do it with a fresh egg.' When I was getting christened, my dad was over the fells playing quoits. They had to go and seek my dad across there. 'The bairn's getting christened.' 'Oh, I forgot, I'll come across.'

Derek Hall

Jubilee Celebrations

The Silver Jubilee celebrations of King George V and Queen Mary early in 1935 was one big affair. They had a chain of bonfires, beacons lit from Lands End to John O'Groats. The first West Stanley Scout group, which I belonged to,

Boys from the First West Stanley Scouts build a beacon from old coal tubs and waste timber from West Stanley Colliery, to celebrate the Silver Jubilee of George V in 1935. The boy on the left is Ernie Cheeseman.

This impressive bonfire was built in West Kyo in 1902, for the Coronation of Edward VIII.

was given the job of erecting one of these beacons on Burn's Pit heap. I think we actually did two per cent of the building, because the group Scout Master worked at Burn's Pit. He contacted the owners of the pit, and all the rotten timbers and pit props and wooden tubs that were no good were stacked up by the men on the heap stead. They did most of the work. We guarded it of course, each night.

Ernie Cheeseman

Bonfire Night

On Bonfire Night, nearly every village, every two or three hundred yards, would have a bonfire, a really big bonfire. They would chop trees down; anything and everything went on the bonfire. Before Bonfire Night you would raid the appropriate village and set their bonfire off a few days before Bonfire Night, oh it was good fun! The bonfires were still burning the next day when we went to school, they were so big.

John Nicholson

Pot Eggs and Varnish

You tossed the coin to see who would hold and who would jarp. If I've lost – I've said heads when it should have been tails – I hold my egg blunt side up. You will use your egg's sharp end, bring it down on mine. If you break the shell of mine you have won and you can take my egg off me. However, if yours breaks then I take the egg off you. Now you'll have heard of pot eggs for bringing clucker hens on, I understand that actually there are some people who have used them so that they win a lot of money. I can't say that that is very true because a pot egg felt different even though it would be decorated as an Easter egg. And there were some magnificent decorations. The other thing was that they would get an egg and varnish it and then decorate it, you know: this sort of thing make it stronger for winning.

Ernie Cheeseman

Streets Full of Eggshells

We used to stand outside till two o'clock in the morning jarping eggs. When the eggs were boiled there was always the hollow part on one side. We used to get boxes of these and the men used to buy a few eggs and they used to stand testing them with their teeth to see if they were hard, then one used to challenge the other that his egg was better than his. Great fun like, you know. Outside the shop used to be all full of eggshells.

Dominic Bove

Egg Rolling

Down the fields was Greenwell Farm. We would go there. There was a field where there was a bank, to roll our paste eggs down. And occasionally we might do a bit of jarping but it was frowned upon because that was what the bad lads used to do. But we used to roll our Easter eggs down like that. And incidentally it was a bit of a torment. Oh, we enjoyed it great, but there was a restraint because we were in our Easter best, which incidentally was your Sunday best for the next twelve months.

Ernie Cheeseman

Six

DOWN THE MINES

The Pit Yard

The countryside was magnificent but my favourite playground was any pit yard. And in those days, it was 'Get away lads, you can't come in', but on a Saturday morning, when the pit was not working but on standby, there was two or three people around there, but the pit was standing idle. And so I would get myself dressed in my best gansey and do my hair, comb it out, and I would go over and inveigle myself, 'Hey mister, can I see your engine?' Well the winding engine man, he'd got nothing to do, he was glad of the company, so that's how I used to have a look round the colliery. And, in fact, in one mine, this was the old vertical single cylinder winding engine, he actually let me drive it. Of course there was nothing in the cage, it was empty going up and down, but he actually let me drive it.

Ernie Cheeseman

Playing on the Tubs

The Beamish Burn Drift, the sets used to come out there, with maybe twenty tubs on, and we used to wait there as kids, then jump on the first few empty ones coming out. There was a man sitting on the back with a piece of steel on a shaft in case it got derailed. He used to shout, 'Get off you little buggers, get off I'll tell your dads!' We used to sit with our backs to him – we knew he dare not stop it. We used to wait until just before the river and jump off and run away. He daren't stop it for his life!

Eddie Nicholson

Boys playing in the tubs of the colliery yard of Beamish Second Pit, *c.* 1960.

Job Choices

In those days there was nothing but pits here. You had only two choices, either pits or, if you could get it, a job in a shop. That's the only choice you had. There was no factories and there was no buses. You had the railway, but of course it was very seldom you got on to the railway. So that was about all you could do.

My father had been working in the Beamish Mary pit. We happened to know the fore-overman, and my father said to him, 'He's talking about wanting to be down the pit. But if he does what I tell him, he'd keep out of it, if he can.' The overman says, 'I'll tell you what I'll do with you, Jack, if he has a mind to come down the pit, I'll take him down and take him in and let him see what pit work is.' And that was what he did. He took me down the shaft and I saw just what pit work was. He said, 'Well, what do you think about that lot?' I said, 'Not very much!' It was a dark hole. We had an over lamp, but that's the only lamp we had in this dark hole. And we went quite a long way in.

Anonymous

You Had to Think about Your Coals

My dad didn't want us to go into the pits, he wanted me to be a slaughter man, like what he used to do, but you just followed your family. Your brother was in the pits, your grandfather, your father, uncles, you more or less followed them. Well I did think about it, aye. But my friends got off school and went into the pits.

So I went down. I fancied being a bricklayer, so I went and I said, 'Is there any vacancies for bricklaying?' He said, 'Son, see that list there? I'll put you on the bottom.' About six month after there was a knock at the door, 'You've got to start apprentice bricklaying on Monday.' At the time, you know, you're the breadwinner of the house – my dad was getting on to retirement age then – and you had to think about your coals, think about your house.

Derek Hall

First Experiences

It was a custom among miners to take their sons with them in the school holidays, I was down maybe a dozen times with my dad over the school holidays, just to get acclimatised to it, you know, the inevitable way of life. But it wasn't the same as the first day by myself, the other times I could grab hold of his hand. Nobody will ever know what I felt like on that pit heap that morning when I went on my own. I was terrified of the place.

I went to a trapdoor. This lad said, 'Make yourself a seat, it'll be a long day.' I got two planks and put them down there, and I just had to open the doors. I found out a long time later this was just a way of getting a new lad acclimatised to the atmosphere of the place, because the pony could get the door open itself! I think I saw the putter three times all day long – a great shadow with his lamp, going by

Beamish Mary Pit, *c.* 1955.

Five pit lads, titled 'the straight banana club', pose for the camera, *c.* 1927. Their lamps and pony whips can be clearly seen.

with his pony ... I walked about that area terrified. I didn't want to make an ass of myself and panic, but nobody knows to this day how I kept a grip on myself. Of course you hadn't to tell anyone you were frightened, they'd've thought you were soft.

Dick Morris

Sitting for Eight Hours

The first job I got was sitting on a seat of some sort knocking what they call the clips off the tubs. I used to sit there with an iron bar and knock that clip off before it went down that decline. Sitting there for eight hours by yourself in the dark, surrounded with mice, you know. Oh what a job. Anyway, I stuck it for a bit and then I came out and that's when I made enquiries for a job in the shop.

Anonymous

Down the Warren Drift

I left school on the Friday, at six o'clock on the morning I was going up to Burnhope. It was a beautiful summer's morning, the birds whistling, it was in July, the skylarks up in the sky, the smell of flowers, and everything. And then, you got to the colliery. And away we went into the Warren drift, that's where the stables was. You had your bait poke in your arm, and your bottle of water or tea in your pocket. And your midgie, that was your light, and you went in. When you went in from the blinding sunshine, you couldn't see a thing. All I could do was follow the noise of people's feet walking in front of me. I couldn't see very well, and the smoke came off these midgies, and there was a torch, and they smoked. But the deputy, he had a safety lamp. I remember sitting down and him talking, I could hear the jangle of ponies coming out of the stable, to go into where they had to work, and eventually there was only me left. When we went in, water dripping down, you were up to your knees in stinking water, and rats – the place was alive with them. However, with using horses on the farm, I was familiar with ponies and that. That didn't bother me. I knocked a nail into a post, and I hung my bait bag on there. And when I went to get it, there was nothing in it; the rats had eaten the bottom out of it. I had nothing to eat all day.

Jack Geddes

A lantern slide depicting miners hewing coal by hand.

Driving the Coals

At the shaft bottom I could walk about without bumping my head on the timbers at all, 'cos it was all nice and high. The next week they sent me to the bank bottom. It took some getting used to going to a place where you were stooped all day long. My head was all chipped with catching the timbers, till I learnt the lesson the hard way. The next day when they sent us down this east side, as they called it, I suppose there must have been a dozen of us sat waiting to get our lamps examined by the deputy, and all of a sudden, unexpectedly, there was a shot fired. I'd never a heard a shot go off before. The whole place shook, you know, my heart jumped – I remembered the Stanley explosion and I thought the whole pit had gone off!

Of course the next week, I was driving the coals. That was champion; I had an oil lamp, I could sit on the limbers to ride in, and sit on the limbers to ride out. I was getting my confidence like the rest of the lads and going about it like an old hand.

That lasted for a couple of weeks and then they sent you somewhere else, to get you acclimatised to being on your own.

Dick Morris

On the Screens

I started on the screens, picking coal. You started at twelve o'clock till half past eight, with twenty minutes off. And it was twenty minutes not twenty-one. And you weren't allowed to go to the toilet more than once a shift. At the time there were three screens going, so you can imagine the clatter. So we developed a deaf and dumb sign. You would pick up and hit any metal. The belt driver would look up and you would point to your bum, 'Can I go to the toilet?' His mouth would go and he would bring his watch out. He would look at it and point. In other words, three minutes you've got to be back again or else. The screens were on stilts, twenty-ton railway trucks had to get underneath them. And you can imagine what a north-eastern wind would do there. In the summer time I used to wear an old jacket, one shirt, a pair of trousers and a pair of boots, nothing else, and the same in the winter time. And all the time there was this belt slowly going past you. Oh dear me and the time absolutely dragged. That first shift was a year and a half!

Jack Geddes

Burning Coals

Granddad Nicholson had a burn up the back of his leg because his overalls caught fire one morning. He was taking burning coals from one locomotive to another one, and it was a windy morning and he had a shovel full of burning coals and he suddenly realised that his overalls were on fire, greasy overalls. He never recovered from that – he had a burn all the way back up of his leg.

John Nicholson

Working with Pug Lime

We used to all meet at the masons' cabin on a morning, and they used to make pug lime. There was plenty of ballast about the pit you see, out of the furnaces. They used to grind it all up. The pug mill was a big pan about seven or eight feet wide, two great big heavy rollers in it – used to put a few shovelfuls of ballast in that pan, and a shovelful or two of ordinary lime, and grind it up. It was grand stuff for building bricks – mortar, before cement come out, was all pug lime; it

A man works with coal tubs at the landing, Morrison Busty Pit, Annfield Plain, *c.* 1952.

set very hard. There was an old chap used to look after it, old Tom Dowsey. When it got properly filled ready to come out, he would get his shovel out, as the thing was going around, and throw it onto the heap like that, and he lost many a shovel you know, it got into the rollers. But never mind, he never took any harm.

Jack Edgell

Shiftwork

Your shifts governed your social life absolutely. No one liked afternoon shifts because you didn't have an evening's entertainment, and no one liked the morning shift because you were that tired you couldn't enjoy your evening. Getting up at quarter past three in the morning. When I got home at one o'clock or something like that I had a bath, because there were no pit head baths, and had a meal. It would then be well after two o'clock so you'd go to bed and you'd probably wake up seven or eight o'clock at night.

Ernie Cheeseman

Pick Sharpening

There was a pick sharpeners' cabin – they used to sharpen the picks what men hewed the coals with. It was a little cabin just on the end, about eight or nine feet square. The pitmen used to bring picks here – they were sent up on the heap, they were all put on a big ring. He got so much wage from the colliery a week, and the pitmen at so much a pick. He had a payment, just coppers you see.

Jack Edgell

Pit Lamps and Gas

We had oil lamps, what they used to call acetylene lamps. The officials had the electric cap lamp. And of course the deputies had what you used to call safety lamps, because they had to test for gas. They pulled the wick down until it was the lowest light that they could get. And the colour of the flame denotes gas.

Robert Gardiner

Rats and Cats

Now my father complained that there were rats in the underground stables – the rats were everywhere and, unfortunately, gnawing into the bins with the horses' corn in. So when our mother cat had kittens, we kept one. He took this tiny little kitten down the pit with him and he used to take its mother down every day, because horses need to be attended to seven days a week. I remember saying, 'How's the kitten dad?' And he said, 'These blessed rats are jumping over him.' Then some three, four, five months later I asked again and he said, 'Oh Tom, he's a wonderful ratter, he's cleared all the rats great.' He was highly delighted. Then one day a huge tomcat came in, sat down in front of the fire. My mother said, 'Where's that strange cat come from?' When my father came in he said, 'Hello Tommy.' That cat had found its way home after more than eighteen months down the pit.

Ernie Cheeseman

Ponies

The duties of a horse keeper were to train the horse as it came down. By jingo that must have been a dreadful experience for the horse. What had to happen was the cage had to be taken out then they would put a horse on its belly and lower it down into the dark abyss. And the horse would be terribly frightened, and it would be taken away into the stables. And of course it had to be trained. By the way, an old hand horse didn't need any light. It knew where to keep its head down and when the end of the shift came. It knew. But a new horse being broken in, you had to be with the horse all the time going down the incline. And what does a frightened horse do but kick?

Ernie Cheeseman

Pit Pony Holidays

I think they kept them down for about six month. Then they might pick six horses to go up you see. And when they were brought to bank they used to take them along to their own colliery fields, and when they got in the fields they were kicking and flinging and enjoying the fresh air again you see. And there was a lot of places round here, and on the way to Leadgate, you could see them jumping about that field. But they'd be up for so many weeks then they'd go back in the pit again. But they got the green choppie and they got the green grass, they got the corn, and they were well fed in the pits you see. So really the life of a pit pony wasn't so bad.

Samuel Jackson

A Good Pony

Pit ponies had a hard life you know. A good pony, he worked two shifts. And a bad one was standing in the stable and never worked. They would take the pony into the stable when he'd finished with his shift; he was fed and watered by the horse keeper. And the next chap that come for his pony, he wasn't supposed to take that one 'cos it had just come in, but when a pony was allotted to him, he'd say, 'I'm not going to take that bugger,' and he'd go and take the good one. And they had little whips – great long thong on them.

Jack Edgell

Three young miners from Wooley Pit, Stanley, enjoy a ride on the pit ponies.

Pit Pony Stables

Every stall had [the horse's] name on, 'Toby', 'Jack', 'Bobby', 'Bob', 'Robert' and so on. And them stables was spotlessly clean, whitewashed you know. The horse keepers were that proud of their stables that they never cared about the inspectors, because it was their job to keep the horses clean and well fed and that, you see. And there was cats in the stables to keep the mice and rats down. They were proper brick-built stables, electric lights right along. And when them horses were finished on a night time, they would turn into this electric light-lit stable, and away along to their own stalls, have a good drink and a good feed, and then after a while they would lie down.

Samuel Jackson

Training as a Bevan Boy

We had a month to six weeks training down a disued mine. It had all the machinery and things but it wasn't very deep, the Morrison Busty, this training section. And it wasn't very dark. It was well lit, electric light, and so it give me no inkling of what was to come. I suppose it was a gradual introduction for these people from London, from Inverness, all over the place who didn't know what a pit was. At least I knew what a pit was. They were going to be introduced to it in as nice a way as possible. So they lit the place up and they made the shaft very shallow. In fact I've heard it said if you were late and you'd missed the cage, you could jump down!

Ronald Barrass

Bevan Boys

They brought the Bevan Boys up to work in the pits, but my brother-in-law, he was called up – he was twenty-one-years-old. It was a funny system, they took lads out the pit to go and fight, and they brought these lads up from London, to work in the pits!

Derek Hall

The Hard Life to Come

After training, you lived in a hostel at Annfield Plain, in round Nissen huts. We all stayed together and we were given exercises. We had to run over these hills away above Annfield Plain. There was boxing lessons for those who wanted to box – all supposed to toughen you up for the hard life to come. You had to obey authority in no uncertain terms. They said you do this, you did that, and you didn't give them too much cheek, because the penalty then was jail. If you didn't go along with them, if you said, 'No I'm not going down there,' then there was no two ways about it, you were jailed.

Ronald Barrass

Paynotes

My father used to bring his paynote home from the pit. Just before I was born they started paying every week. Before that it was every fortnight. My wife's eldest sister was born on what you call a pay Friday, which was considered to be very lucky. The week that they didn't get paid was a 'baff' Friday, so there was pay Friday and 'baff' Friday.

The paynote was a long document; on the top was his name, works number and then the total amount of what he had earned. There was of course about five bob taken off for his 'Lloyd George' – that was an insurance stamp. All the doctors in the area, their names were on it. Now my mother liked Doctor Fox so a penny was put against his name. A bit further down there was the district nurse, a penny. There was the cottage hospital, a penny, Newcastle Royal Victoria Infirmary, a penny. So for a matter of about five pence we had a National Health Service, back in the 1920s.

Ernie Cheeseman

Colliery First Aid

There was an ambulance house here as well, a cabin, and a cupboard with all sorts of equipment, and they had a brick out in the wall with a little door in it for keeping morphia. If the chap was hurt in the pit they used to bring him into this ambulance room, and lay him on the table. They had hot water; they would wash him and keep him easy till the colliery ambulance came to take him away. That horse ambulance was stopped in here. But they got a motor ambulance after that, an Austin. I used to sometimes take it to the RVI. I often used to make splints here at the yard, and they used to get lectures in the ambulance house, for anyone that fancied taking up ambulance work.

Jack Edgell

Tobacco Cure

In them days nobody down the pit had a helmet unless he was an official. This chap he was a coal hewer and a stone fell and cut his head. Do you know what he did? This chap peeled some of his tobacco off and stuck it on his head. Did him good. They must have been tough!

Robert Gardiner

Seven

TOUGH TIMES

A Lanchester Character

Tom Rut, he was a character in Lanchester. He looked very tall but was tubby, round. He always had these sort of greasy dark trousers and black coat on. He would pick everything up, a cigarette packet or sweet papers, or anything like that; he would gather them up and push them in his pockets. You would think he was a very corpulent fellow, but eventually he entered the workhouse. He must have been stuffed with a mass of papers, all sorts of rubbish, sweet papers, cigarette packets, anything he could pick up. And he died in there.

Jack Geddes

Dole School

About the second week in January I was marched up with my mother and enlisted in the Stanley Dole School. If you had had a job and through no fault of your own you became redundant you would have to go to the Dole School to keep your benefit, to keep your 'Lloyd George' stamp. Coming from day school you went if you wanted to. But I was made to by my mother! The school was held in a number of buildings owned by the West Stanley Co-operative Society. Some people stayed in the Dance Hall, there were trestle tables put up there, did arithmetic or mechanical drawing. Or you could go out of the building along the road southwards, to the woodworking and metal working shop.

Now here is a peculiar thing. The instructors there were not allowed to instruct. They could answer questions that you asked correctly, but they couldn't give you information! The reason being that you had to have an apprenticeship as a carpenter before you were taught anything – the unions prevented that. The same

The inhabitants of Lanchester Workhouse, with a nurse.

with metalwork and what have you. But anyway there was magnificent work turned out. I built myself a dog kennel. I think you could have got a car into it, but there we are.

Ernie Cheeseman

Stone Breaking at the Workhouse

At eight o'clock on every night but Sunday, the tramps would line up at the police station to get a ticket for a night's lodgings in the workhouse. They would get a bath, and some sort of food, and then the next morning they would be up at breakfast and they had to put a day in breaking stones. There was a big break yard, a big pile of stones – the limestone was brought into the stone yard in big lumps. And they had these little hammers, breaking them up for road making. And then when it comes maybe five o'clock they were finished, they would get a meal, and then move on to Chester-le-Street workhouse for the next night, that's how they lived, these tramps. Rather than apply to the board of guardians they'd just tramp round from one workhouse to another. There was a saw bench, and a lot of railways sleepers used to be delivered to there, and there was a misfortunate chap used to saw these railways sleepers into six-inch lengths. The inmates used to have to chop this up into sticks for fire. The more responsible ones among them had a machine for wiring them into bundles, and all those were sold by the workhouse you see.

Jack Geddes

Running Barefoot

That was a period when I had boots for Sunday only! I ran around in bare feet. It was partly through choice. I said, 'Mam, if I wear my boots out, I'll have nothing to wear for Sunday, so can I go around in my bare feet?' Well she wasn't sure, but everybody else was so we started running about in our bare feet.

Ernie Cheeseman

The Pit Buzzers Stop

The Hedley went 'wug, wug, wug'. The Billy 'cong, cong, cong' and the Billy pit generator 'ticker, ticker, ticker' and so on, and you could tell by the different pitch of the buzzers as they blew. Incidentally on a New Year's evening when twelve o'clock came all the buzzers blew in the whole area. Getting on for ten of them I think, within ten minutes of course. But in the Depression, when the pits were working one, two and three days a week, they used to blow the buzzers in the early evening prior to when the pit was off and they would listen and they would know by the pitch of the buzzer which pit it was, 'no more work until tomorrow.'

Ernie Cheeseman

Keeping the Fires Burning During the Strike

It was all right for the first fortnight or three weeks. Our main problem was getting coals to keep our fires going, miners' fires were always big fireplaces. We put bricks in to try and reduce the size of the fireplaces on each side, but we'd been so well used to one side boiling the water, the other side for the oven, they couldn't put bricks in because you had no other means of cooking except the oven. They had a pair of tongs to take the hot bricks out when you wanted to use the oven, and blow it with the blower, then put the bricks back again to try to keep a bit of fire going.

Dick Morris

Going Hungry

If I had been as observant then as I am now I would have seen how the weight must have dropped off my parents, because there was very little food left in the house. We used to go to school, not for nine o'clock but for eight o'clock. We would be crocodile marched down to the Miners' Hall down at the bottom of South Moor, where soup kitchens were put on. And breakfast would be a bowl of gruel and a wedge of bread, which would make about four reasonable slices, you know. I always remember sticking that lump of bread up my gansey and having the gruel. And the same at dinner time, it would be broth, vegetable broth – no meat at all. Whacking great chunks of bread up the gansey – for my parents. My brother used to do the same.

Ernie Cheeseman

Digging the Hills

My God, getting the coal out of that hill was tough work, we never realised what a load of coal meant till we had to get them ourselves. To the gaffer's credit he did agree to open the seam officially in the end, but the risks that people took to open that hillside was nobody's business. There was quite a lot of lads hurt, they were digging in holes, going too far in without any timber and getting buried. My brothers and I were digging in one place one Saturday there, and somebody shouted, 'Dicky, come on over, there's a lad buried here and we divven't know where to start.' The whole bank side had crumbled on top of him. When we got him released the doctor came and had a look at him and says, 'He's dead.' We scraped around his face and got his head released, and I'm sure he wasn't crushed or anything like that, just suffocated. We put him on a stretcher and took him home.

Dick Morris

They were Breaking the Law

There was a policeman called Ward. In the 1926 strike, the men knew where the coal was, the seams on the Yew Tops. Ward used to sit on the Yew Tops and wait for the men struggling there with this bag of coal, and he would take his knife and slit it open. He was a kindly man, mind, to the children. Used to put the fear of God into us sometimes but he was a kind man deep down. Of course they were breaking the law – they could have been killed, digging into the side there, because they had no support for the roof; they were just digging for coal for the fire.

Ethel Murray

Four Bags of Coal

They built a drift mine down in the side of the dene and they put this big wire rope up from the top end right across and it was shackled round this big tree at the bottom. Then they had a running pulley going up and down and you had to go in and dig your own coal. I remember this day my father had been in and he had dug four bags of coal out, and he gave one to the fellas who were running the pulley and he gets the other three and he puts them on his bike, over the wheel like and through the crossbar, another one on the top on the handlebars. He said, 'We might just get this last one on.' He put the last one on and the wheel bent and he finished up on the two forks! Our lad ran home to get the two boneshakers and wheel them up.

Anonymous

The Aftermath

There was a chap had a butcher's shop in South Moor. He joined the Special Police to fight the miners. The people of South Moor boycotted his shop and he went bankrupt. You see you've got to be very careful how you treat people. You've got to be careful. He thought he was all right joining the Special Police but he was wrong.

Robert Gardiner

What a Melee

I don't know why they picked on us, but a platoon of troops came marching in with rifles and bayonets. They were trying to cow us I think. And a squadron of police – about twenty of them – come up behind them, and they had great long truncheons, about eighteen inches, and they had all these on their shoulders. The pit gates were just at the bottom of our street, just across the road, and all the men were gathered around the pit gates. Us lads, we were hiding behind the walls. And the women were standing there, looking about like. I can remember this copper standing up and reading this notice out. I didn't know it was the Riot Act. In the end like they suddenly just charged. They didn't say nowt they just charged, the lot of them, shouting and yelling their bloody heads off. And there was my father, my uncles; they all had bloody clothes posts which meant they could hit the copper before the copper could hit them. Oh what a melee. God the batons was crunching. There were fellas had pit props, never mind bloody clothes props. We were hoying stones. Because it was an accepted way of life, that was your entertainment, stone fights street to street. It ranged back and forward for about three hours. But in the end we got on top of them, oh aye. We all got stuck in. We actually drove them out the village, but they were back the next day with twice as many! There was quite a few put in jail and all.

Anonymous

An Explosion

The Morrison had the fire you know, the explosion, at the pit, in Annfield Plain. My dad was a miner and when I heard it on the wireless I didn't know whether my dad was on that shift. I went flying down from Annfield Plain to South Moor, and here's my dad and mam in bed! And I says, 'Dad, there's been an explosion at the Morrison North.' So he got up then, like, to come to the pit. And Mr Bramley came up to me at the kiosk and he says, 'Ella, if anybody comes from the pit and they want any cigarettes, it doesn't matter how many they want, let them have them.'

Rachel Smith

We Had to Get There

I was on my hands and knees bathing in front of the fire when Mrs Porter, our neighbor, shouted across, 'The Burnses pits' gone off, you can see the smoke coming out the shaft!' And my dad said we had to get there. We were only twelve yards from the sleeper fence with the railway running from all the pits west right away to Annfield Plain, it ran through all the gardens. We climbed on the back of the empty wagons, and in about half an hour we were up there at Stanley. We got the last set before the banks closed because of the pit disaster.

Dick Morris

Rushing from School

We were just coming out of school at ten to four I remember. There was a lot of smoke and us lads rushed across the fields and of course the whole area was alerted. And when we came back my father said, 'You're not going over there any more,' and he wouldn't allow us back to the Burns Pit to see what was going on.

Anonymous

At the Pit Head

When we got there, there were quite a few people there but not as many as began crowding in as we stood there. We were standing underneath the screens watching the shaft, and the smoke was still coming out of the shaft. There was nothing anybody could do; the police were there to try to keep a gangway for the rescue people. Anyway, we'd been there two hours, they got a cage to the bottom, hosepipes laid down the shaft to put the fires out. By another half hour

Two miners in their protective sinkers headgear, shortly after the West Stanley Pit disaster of 1909. They are Bill McKeand, the first man to reach the Busty Seam, and Tom Swinburn, the first to reach the Brockwell Seam.

the first rescue people began to explore from the shaft bottom down, and we just stood there, the women crying, their men in the pit, that sort of thing. It took from about half seven when we got there till eleven before they brought anybody out, one or two survivors. It was getting dark, people had to walk home, my father said to his brother, 'I think its time we went, Jim, we have to go to work tomorrow morning just the same.'

Dick Morris

The Rescue Team

On Wednesday at four o'clock in the afternoon I went down with a party to see what we could do. When we come up they were asking us questions, 'What did you see?' I said we went down to look for live 'uns, not dead 'uns. It was live 'uns we were looking for, the dead 'uns was no good to us, were they? The place was all smashed tubs, horses, lads – they were all bashed into each other at the shaft bottom. At the shaft bottom you see there was iron rails, bent, that's where the explosion was. And the men, they were just sitting round, some of them with not a mark on them, sitting there, couldn't stir, couldn't speak, couldn't nod. They were all black with the nasty stuff, black damp they call it, that killed them. You just touch them and they fell over. So we had to straighten them out and wrap them with canvas. Then the rescue party come in and took them out, got them to the bank as soon as possible. But mind there were others smashed to bits. Depends where these fellows was to catch the bump, see.

Jack McGregor

Before the Funerals

The undertaker wasn't putting the coffin lids on until the last minute and people were going round the houses, looking into the coffins. I said to my father, 'Why don't they kick them out, dad, it's like they're ghouls, out of one house and into the next one just peering into the coffins.' He said, 'It's curiosity. I suppose they've never seen anything like this before.' We tried to get into the churchyard but it was impossible, we couldn't get anywhere near the churchyard, we stood on the road leading down to it. We just simply had to stand there watching them carrying the coffins in, and they never got them buried the rest of that day because half of them were still stretched back up the street. Men were fainting because they couldn't carry the banner, all standing. I will never forget it, seeing the people carry the coffins and putting them down, all the way down that main street in Stanley there. It was heart-rending.

Dick Morris

Locals gather at the pit head, waiting for the rescuers to bring news from West Stanley Pit.

A Butcher's Shop

There was funerals on the Friday, funerals on the Saturday, funerals on the Sunday and Monday. But the Sunday one, oh, there was thousands and thousands there. Ever so many lads I knew was lost in the explosion. There was some had no legs, and some one arm, and some one leg, such as that. And there was many a chap whose legs belonged to another man in one coffin. See, they didn't know what to do, they were all blown to bits, but when they got them into the shed at the top of the pit heap they started, you know, to put them into coffins, such as that. Well, some men had three legs. It was a butcher's shop. They couldn't tell who they were …

Jack McGregor

Flowers for the Grave

I watched them digging trenches one morning when I was coming back past the church. I went to the funerals on the Sunday and Monday; the boss let us all off and it was a day and a half. I used to go and put a few wild flowers on those poor lads' graves, those that didn't have any flowers on. I couldn't afford the good flowers.

Eliza Brown

Mourners line the streets during the funeral of the victims of the West Stanley Pit disaster.

The last of the victims of the disaster go to their graves.

Air-raid shelters in Joicey Square, Stanley, in 1939. The larger buildings in the background are the Pavilion Theatre and the Salvation Army Citadel.

Twizell Bomb

That night that bomb went off – Twizell wood was straight opposite, there used to be a big bridge across it at Twizell woods, all the clothes out of all the drawers and the wardrobes, they was all over the trees. It was an awful sight. And mind if that bomb had gone off just a little bit sooner there was a northern bus just went up Beamish Road, and there would have been more casualties. The cobbling stones off the railway wall, great big ones, thick and solid, they were all tossed onto the middle of the road, and I know one man that was killed with one hitting him. It was terrible. The night after that there was a lot of sightseers come down in the buses from Stanley and places – I say sightseers but I know there was some came to see if their relations was alright at Beamish.

Ethel Short

Beamish Blitz

Mr Tate was killed in the Blitz – there was a blitz in Beamish here and eight people was killed. My father was a special constable and he was up on the main road; there was an unexploded bomb in the house, it had been there all night – the raid was at night but the bomb went off at nine in the morning and blew the place to pieces. We were the only ones left in the street; everyone went to live with their relations. My wife and I used to sleep in the cupboard under the stairs for safety.

Jack Edgell

Delivering War Notices

I once remember in Knowle Street, a woman was in bed with a child, and I went this morning with a letter and I knew it was bad news. I said, 'Good morning,' and she said, 'Good morning. Have you got me a letter from my man?' I said, 'I have. I don't know whether it's good or bad news but open it while I'm here.' She opened it and the screams from that woman was ridiculous. I said, 'Listen, take the baby and sit down there and I'll get some help.' I went down the back steps; that was the only time I left my bag, I was scared stiff. I went down there and along to Pompy Clark's big gate. I had to bray as hard as I could and he came to the door in his night attire. 'Haway,' he says, 'I'll come,' and he went as he was, in just his pyjamas and a big, long shirt, and he went along there in his bare feet to help that woman. That woman was in a desperate state. She said, 'He's never seen this bairn.' I said, 'Never mind, pet, the Lord will look after you.' Well, you don't know what to do, being young you see, but we did the best we could for them. There was many a time when we got back we were cross-questioned why we were late.

Eliza Brown

Eight

AT SCHOOL AND CHURCH

Nursery School

The teacher was ever so nice. She was pleasant, very pleasant. But she seemed to be so big to me – of course I'd just be a tiny tot then. And she wore black. And I remember the very first day I went, she wanted me to get onto the horse, the little rocking horse. And we played with coloured sticks, making images and things like that.

Anonymous

Tin and Ash

I went to West Pelton School. In those days the infant school was a tin school, and they had this horrible ash playground, and if you fell down you scraped your knees. And I remember starting school because I could read quite well, and I was very bored at the beginning, because they were teaching me to read and I could already read. I was there until I was eleven and then I went to Alderman Wood School at Stanley.

Irene Wilson

Classrooms and Desks

The desks were two together, with lids on the desk and just an ordinary seat with the back on to join the two up, you know. They had a greeny shade, I think. All the doors were dark green. The hallway was dark green paint. I don't remember any pictures, but there were maps pinned up. We were sat with our back to the walls, looking at the blackboards and the doors out to the hallway. There were

A group of children at Stanley nursery school, photographed for the *Durham Advertiser* in 1949.

these partitions down each side between classes – not a wall, just a partition. I remember once when it fell over. I don't think anyone was hurt but it was a lucky thing that they weren't!

Mary Allinson

Sitting on Hot Pipes

I remember skipping along to school early and going into the classroom, putting out the exercise books, pens and inkwells, and you always chose a nice pen for yourself. And for that week we got a halfpenny each. In the winter time we used to have to plodge through snow. We used to think it would be a good idea to take our sandwiches and cans of cocoa, and Ganny – as we used to call her – would keep it hot until we went at lunchtime to go and collect it. And then, when we took our sandwiches and cocoa, we would just sit in the cloakroom on pipes, hot pipes.

Anonymous

Cocoa Cans in Winter

There was no meals at school in them days, the children had to bring them; they'd bring cans of cocoa and the schoolmaster used to let them stand them near the fire. There were great big fireplaces in West Pelton School. The master was very kind, he used to let them go home on a winter, on snow days, because they had a long walk right through Beamish, right to the Shepherd and Shepherdess, right down the forges. And I mean, there were some little tots used to come. There was no buses for it back then.

Ethel Short

Pens and Slates

You were lucky if you got a good pen nib. The ink used to occasionally get spilled too. Of course in the beginning we used to use slates, you know. Horrid things, they used to squeak with the scraping of the pencil on. Eee gosh when I think about it! We sometimes used to spit to wipe it off. We always used to have a rag, bring your own rag of course.

Mary Allinson

Trouble with Words

I look back on my schooldays as being horrible because today they would have diagnosed me as being dyslexic. I used to get things the wrong way round. Boot lace was lace boot. Eggcup was cupegg and things like that. There was one teacher, she did try to help me. The others were, 'You stupid little boy,' and 'You careless boy, you've spelled it right up there but it's wrong here.' And I can actually remember my mam taking me to the doctors. I think he gave me a bottle of sugared water. I think it was beyond him as well. But that coloured my schooldays.

Ernie Cheeseman

Cookery

We girls used to do cookery lessons; the boys must have got drawing lessons. Because we used to take a whole afternoon for cookery, we had to go to South Moor. We had to walk from East Stanley to South Moor. It was a long way for kids.

Mary Allinson

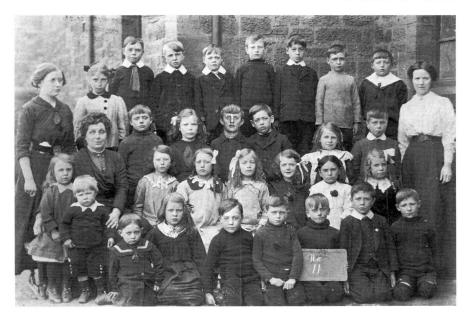

A class photograph from East Stanley School.

Old-Fashioned Pinnies

We used to wear the old-fashioned pinnies with the things on the top, cast downs, you know. Well, they were all old-fashioned but they were clean. We never took any harm. We had Miss Maclaren and Miss Tate but Miss Maclaren would think nothing of pulling you by the ears if you did anything wrong. She was an awful woman.

Lydia Hanley

A Bad Lad

There was this chap, Jimmy Tinnions. I don't know why, but he always bullied me. And this particular day I said, 'I've had enough.' Looking back it was more by good luck than good management. I lashed out at him and bloodied his nose, of which he immediately started crying, as bullies do. Unfortunately for me who should be looking out of the window but Mr Lawson. Bang, bang, bang, bang on the window. Pointed to me, crooked his finger, and I always remember five. Five on each hand. My hands, oh! And I daren't say to my mam when I got home, 'Look what the teacher has done,' because all she would say was, 'You must have been a bad lad to get it and you'll get a good hiding off me now!' But funnily enough Jimmy Tinnions and I became great friends after that!

Ernie Cheeseman

Boys and their teacher, Harold Seccombe, in a classroom at Annfield Plain Boys' School.

Rambles

The furniture had drawers in the bottom, that's where they kept little bits of fossils and things like that, for lessons. And at Lanchester we often used to go out on rambles in the countryside, and we'd look out for things like that, you see, and wild flowers, gather them and press them. It was a good school.

Jack Geddes

Scarlet Fever

I went to West Pelton School until I was eleven. This was the tin school for the juniors, there would be about four classes there and then you moved over the road to the big school and you stayed there until you were fourteen. Now the year I should have sat the eleven plus, we all had scarlet fever. I was in hospital and I came out and the others all went in one after another and then they took me back in because I was the carrier. But the teacher used to send me all the papers, and I used to do the papers at home.

Iris Summers

A class of children at West Pelton School, *c.* 1912.

Flat on His Back in the Gangway

On the Friday afternoon we used to be able to get a book out the library for half an hour and read it. The teacher was sitting on a chair, there was a big stove and this stove had a big fire guard round it, and there was a chest. There was a girl in front of me called Violet Hamilton. I was busy reading this book, it was *Wallace the Bear Hunter*, and I was enjoying it. And Violet Hamilton gave a squeak, and when she squeaked I looked up, and he looked up. So I thought, I'm not going to let him give me the stick, I haven't done anything, so when I got up, I got in between this fire guard and this piece of furniture. Well he daren't strike down on it, he wasn't a very powerful fellow and I was a tough little guy, and he pulled and pulled and pulled to try and pull me out, but he couldn't. But I was beginning to tire a bit there, and I thought, next time he pulls me, I'll come out, and I did. He didn't expect that, and he went flat on his back in the gangway, and I ran out.

Jack Geddes

Empire Day

We had a big sports day and we used to have a band. And the band went first and then we had a procession round the village. And then they came into a field at the back to be judged, fancy dress. And that was the Pageant of the Empire.

Mr and Miss Bell

I Ran out Many a Time

At Lanchester I left at standard 6, I made no progress. The teacher that taught standard 5, 6 and 7, he was a proper snob, miner's children were of a very low character as far as he was concerned. He was more in favour of the farmer class and the sons and daughters of those that had country jobs. When the others had the ability, he didn't want to recognise it, you see. And I was always of a very determined character and he resented that, you see. That's why I ran out of that school many a time.

Jack Geddes

Hand Inspection

Every morning you had a cold wash. You went down the yard and you put your head under the tap. You always had your head more or less shaved with the shears, with a little weeny top. You always had a cold wash under that tap and then you made your way to school. And when you got to school they used to line you up in the schoolyard, hands out, and they would inspect your hands, and then they would check your neck and check your ears and if you had any muck anywhere

Exercising in the yard of Annfield Plain Boys' School, *c*. 1930.

– you were always fighting and clagging about back and forward between the school – they would just grab you by the ear and they would drag you along to the washhouse and you would have another cold wash in there and all!

Anonymous

Love Feast

When I was three years of age, my mother took me to what was called a Love Feast. It was a form of sacrament. The steward of the church brought water in a loving cup and everybody had to have a drink of water. After that there was a plate of biscuits brought round, and you had to have a portion of the biscuits. And a boy of three, I was always hungry, with not enough to live on you know, and I grabbed the biscuits! My mother was disgusted with me, but she soon got OK again.

Arthur Gowland

A Christening Custom

I was walking past St George's Church at South Moor on a weekday and out came a party of people in their Sunday best no less. No one, but no one used their Sunday best other than on a Sunday – so I didn't know why they should be in Sunday best. This huge – to me, a little boy – foreboding man came across and gave me some sweets, a packet of goodies, cakes, orange, apple and a slice of Christmas cake of all things – Christmas cake! These people were mad, absolutely! I now know that it wasn't Christmas cake, it was Christening cake, and that a little girl had been christened and that I was the first little boy they came across after the christening. If I'd been a little girl I wouldn't have got that.

Ernie Cheeseman

Sunday School Anniversary

The Sunday School Anniversary was the highlight of the year in the village. You got a packed house, and it was quite a lengthy service, a lot of children took part. They recited portions of scripture, which they had committed to memory, and they recited portions of the catechism. There was the odd solo sang, if they could get the kiddies to sing, they sang together with the choir, a number of hymns. As time went on I became Sunday School superintendent, I had the job of collating the programme for the Sunday School anniversary, find the pieces of poetry, decide how much scripture should be said. The catechism became unpopular; it was difficult to find two people to stand and one give the question and the other the answer. Then we got to the greater incorporation of the choir who began giving song services, a demonstration, it was a musical affair with often a model as the centre point, the building of a church, of a cross, of a sword. I remember I made a very large sword, about six foot high, and painted it with gold paint. These demonstrations, as they came to be known, were very popular and drew the people in.

Anonymous

Methodist Meetings

Every Whit Sunday and Monday there were special meetings on the Yew Tops, camp meetings. There would be a lorry there brought from Mr Sid Young's farm, near the chapel. The speaker would stand on this lorry and he would have a congregation of something like two to three hundred. It was a beauty spot and the people used to throng to this place to see the marvellous view from the Yew Tops. And it was well published in the newspapers, the success of these meetings. One of the outstanding speakers was a miner from West Pelton called Mr Tom Lowry. He was a self-educated man, he did attend school a while but he was a reader and he was a marvellous chap. And there was a little portable organ, though it wasn't always used.

Arthur Gowland

A chapel congregation.

Harvest Festival

Harvest festivals were a great do. Jonathan Walker and his wife always took a pride in putting blackberries in the dishes and setting out the harvest festival. And people were great givers; there was always plenty, you know. It was lovely, loads of flowers, and they used to set it out beautifully. The farmers gave generously of wheat, a sheaf of wheat – in fact for years there was two loaves, bread fashioned as a stook of wheat used to be brought out every year. And Hogsby's, the farmers, I think they made the little haystack, all nice on the top, weaved. They used to make corn dollies as well, they were quite good. It was a great occasion. And there always the concert on the Saturday evening, great goings-on, we all enjoyed that.

Ethel Murray

The Blacksmith Preacher

There was one chap, the village blacksmith, Mr George Hunter, he was a Sunday School superintendent and he was a very strict sabbatarian. This preacher came and he had a Sunday paper. He hung his jacket on the peg and the Sunday paper was sticking out and the puritanical blacksmith came – he just took that, put it in the fire and burnt it. Well, that caused a bit of a commotion. The fellow didn't let him know, he didn't ask for it, because he knew he'd done wrong in his opinion. But it caused a lot of argument. One set of people said, 'He shouldn't have done this on the Sabbath day,' and the others said, 'Well it wasn't his to burn, he stole the thing, it wasn't his property.' I remember that – it went on for weeks you know.

Arthur Gowland

Sunday School

Mrs Bartle was my Sunday School teacher and I did enjoy listening to her read out the Bible (most kids you'd think would be bored stiff with that sort of thing). Mrs Bartle used to read it out and Mr George Hunter would be walking up and down the aisle to see that we were all paying attention. We would sing a hymn and there would be a lesson and a prayer, one or two hymns. After that we had the Sunday School treat, a bag of sticky buns and seed cake. They organised little races for us with a little prize at the end of it, and it was quite nice in that field behind the chapel, we thought it was great those days because we didn't get very far.

Ethel Murray

Stitching Quilts

At Beamish Chapel they were working for some fund and the ladies used to make quilts. I remember that quite vividly, going with my grandmother to stitch these quilts and I used to thread the needle for them. I did so much that they made me a little quilt for my doll's cradle!

Mary Ratcliffe

That was Sunday

For church we wore the best clothes we had. Mother bought me and my sister some cream coats for the summer, and she remembers grandma had said to her, 'Poor soul, having to watch those two children with cream coats on going through the wood!' That was when I was quite little, but that's what we had to do to get to church. But then we got back again in time for dinner, mother had it ready for when we came in. Sunday School started again at two o'clock. Father was a Sunday School teacher, he took us back again. Then we had tea and had to be back at church for six o'clock and sit through there until about eight. We had long sermons in those days, and walk all the way back again! It was bed time by the time we got back. That was Sunday!

Mrs Race

Wesleyans and Primitive Methodists

The deputies, the overman, the keekers, the token cabin man and of course all the clerks in the colliery offices, they were a strata above the ordinary working man. And they went to the Wesleyan chapel. If you were a working man you were a dataller, in other words you went to the Primitive Methodists. And of course these lay preachers would invariably be something official at the pit. More often than not, if he was a deputy he would be a Wesleyan lay preacher. It was different politics as well. The Wesleyan would be yellow whilst the Primitive Methodist, of course, would be red.

Ernie Cheeseman

Christmas at the Chapel

The chapel was decorated with holly and ivy, and streamers and tinsel and bells, paper bells. And of course the Senior Guild had a do, and the young people of the chapel had their do at Christmas, and the Ladies' Pleasant Hour took the

New Year for their do. There was bran tubs, and a fish pond – there was a screen around this barrel and you put your fishing rod over and somebody round there put a gift on, for your penny.

Ethel Murray

Easter Best

Now on Easter Sunday out came the best, for the Easter Parade. You would probably go to chapel early and stand outside to see them coming down – all the women with their new hats and the young girls with their new frocks and we lads with our new suits and our knees scrubbed clean and our socks pulled up properly. And we would all go into the chapel.

Ernie Cheeseman

We Used to Go out Singing

On Christmas morning we used to go out singing. We used to meet in the vestry at twelve o'clock and there would be about thirty or forty of us with one clarinet and about six violinists. We used to set off about twelve, come back at seven in the morning and there would be somebody who'd kindly present a ham, it would be boiled, sliced up, sandwiches and coffee, tea, whatever. Sometimes we were rained off and we couldn't play the violins, but we used to stick it out till seven o'clock in the morning.

Arthur Gowland

Funeral Bidders

Bidders used to come around, knocking at the doors, with a kind invitation to attend the funeral of so and so, and kindly invited back to tea. They used to bring the coffins outside in them days, put them on two chairs, and they would form a ring and sing and read a verse of scripture or a prayer or something like that. Then get them onto their shoulders, put them into the hearse and away.

The bidders wore ordinary clothes, but they were always at the funeral, they would walk behind the coffin. If there was a band it would be at the front – I've played at many a one, carried many a one, and the people would be walking behind.

Mr Huscroft

The Colliery Hearse

When grandfather was at the Shepherd and Shepherdess they had a hearse house, they used to keep the hearse there. The key was kept at the Shepherd and Shepherdess. It was for people who had worked at the collieries – they had their own hearse. The cart men at the collieries used to drive it; I've seen it several times out on the road with a coffin in. After a funeral the cart man had to go and wash it out, see it was clean again for the next time. He had to call at the Shepherd and Shepherdess and get the key, and after the key they gave him a glass of whiskey, which were threepence in those days, and after he brought back the key he got another glass.

Jack Edgell

The Frightfullest Thing

In 1910, the colliery bought a big old hearse, and if the family were very hard up they allowed them this hearse. It had glass sides and it would be drawn by horses. It was the frightfullest thing you ever saw – it was just a hearse, but it had eight great big dollies, made of feathers. When you were a child, the whistling of the wind in the feathers would make you run. We were terrified of that, the noise and the whistling as it came down Beamish Road. And that was used for funerals at West Pelton Church.

Ethel Short

South Moor undertaker, Mr Rainbow, on his horse-drawn hearse.

A Child's Funeral

If there was a child born dead, the village midwife would carry the coffin under her cape. I've seen two of them go to the church to bury the child, just a little coffin, carry it to the churchyard to be buried. After that a lot of the hearses had a place on the front to put the children in; if they were a bit older, or too heavy to carry, there was a little box on the front of the hearse.

Jack Edgell

Nine

COUNTRY LIFE

A Good Bank for Sledging

We couldn't wait for winter to come round to get out in the snow. The snow was up to your knees, and you didn't think it was bad, you thought it was great. Our parents might have thought they were bad winters but we didn't. We used to sledge from the Shepherd and Shepherdess down Hammer Square Bank. That was a good bank for sledging then, with plenty of turns and bends and twists.

Eddie and John Nicholson

Above & opposite Two views of the deep snowdrifts which formed on the Co–op Bank, Dipton, in January 1963.

Minnow Catching

There was other laddies besides me and we would all get together, playing, kicking a ball about or something like that. And then we would get into the river, maybes learn to swim – it was quite safe where we were, it wasn't very deep. And of course there used to be little fish in the river, we called them minnows. We used to make a little pool away from the river, and when we had catched them we used to put them in the pool, and then set them away again.

And there was a field where it used to be like a meadow, full of flowers. And we used to all get in there and sit making daisy chains or bouquets with the flowers. Mother would give us a bottle of ginger beer, a stotty cake, sandwich, and then we gan away for the day, come back at night after the sun had gone down.

Joseph French

Damming the River

All the lads from the street, about five or six of us, we would get all the wood out of the forest, all the dead wood like. We would interlace it all together with twigs and dig the clay up and clag the clay on until we had a space sealed off, about two and a half feet deep, you know. We could swim in that then at that age, no problem.

And there was a lot of fish in that river, trout. We used to catch the fish, stick them on the end of a forked stick. We used to get a coat and run them to the side and hoy them onto the bank – use the coat as a net. We'd gut them first, naturally, then stick them on the end of a stick and then stick them in the cinders and let them cook, and then we used to eat them!

Anonymous

Bird Nesting

We used to go bird nesting. I'm sure it wasn't illegal then. Partridges would lay ten or twelve eggs. We would take the partridge eggs home because they were just small eggs, and my mother used to break them into a pan, twelve partridge eggs, and we used to eat them. I don't think we particularly liked them but it was just the sense of adventure, and we didn't think we were doing any wrong taking the birds' eggs.

John Nicholson

The First Violets

When we were living in Twizell, I used to go through the woods in the morning to catch the eight o'clock train with a friend who lived in the village. We used to go through the woods together, which, when I look back now, I think it was rather dark, in the winter time. But I have some lovely memories of that, we used to stop on the way to pick flowers, I used to love flowers. We always knew where the first violets were, where the first flowers were.

Irene Wilson

Swinging over the River

The first time I was sent to Sunday School with Harold Jobson, I must have been about four. I had my brand new second-hand suit on which I think my mother had bought from Joe Secombe. And Harold said to me when we got to the church, 'There's a nice swing down the Forges over the river, we can go down there instead of going to Sunday School?' I said, 'All right.' So we went down the Forges and we went across the burn on the swing, and of course who fell in? I did. I was too scared to go home so I went to my uncle's, and he looked at me and he said, 'Come and get dry by the fire.' He gave me three ha'pence for my bus fare to go down so I wouldn't have to walk down with my wet clothes on, and with one of Annie's cakes inside me. I was ever so late back!

John Williamson

The Deer Park

I remember the deer park very well; there was a lot of deer in there, red deer. They used to frighten the life out of me in the dark, they would fight and their horns would clatter together, you could hear them. There was a very high wall built right along – it seemed high to me, as a nipper. And of course the road then was a dirt road; there was no tarmac down there till the NCB took it over. That burn was clear water; you could see the pebbles on the bottom of the water, but not now.

Ethel Murray

A New World

I really couldn't imagine what a beautiful place this was when I landed by train in the Lintzgreen station: it was absolutely beautiful. All around I saw woodlands

Beamish Hall deer park, *c.* 1940.

and fields, hills and valleys, and I thought I'd come into a new world. I took to nature straight away. And if there was any spare time after school I was down the woods and down the fields searching for Mother Nature; I went nearly every day if the weather was fine. And I found out that I could soon get close to animals and close to birds by keeping quiet if I spotted anything, and they would come close to me to see what I was doing.

Samuel Jackson

Pinching Turnips

I remember my mother once sending me down the railway line, just down over the crossing gates. She said, 'Go and get a turnip and if anybody stops you' – because the policeman was always coming by on his bike – 'just say, "I'm just going to eat it".' My mother sent us to pinch a turnip down the line! I don't know why because we had turnips in the garden!

We used to spend all day playing in the woods. If you got hungry you used to pinch a turnip from the farmer's field. You picked it up by the leaves and you knocked it off the corner of a fence which knocked the roots off, then you'd peel it with your teeth. They were called 'snaggers', you ate the turnip on the hoof, lovely!

There was always a gap in the hedge, where there was a semi-circle in the field, where everyone pinched the turnips in the field. The farmers knew what was going on because every one used to do it.

John and Eddie Nicholson

The Money Hills

We used to go blackberrying down in what you call the 'Bottoms' at Beamish, down into the ravine. And we used to roll over the Money Hills, pretending that we were looking for the money that the Romans had left behind. A really lovely childhood, in that sort of way.

Irene Wilson

Fetching Milk

I had to go down before I went to school and get the milk. I had three cans, a three-gill and a normal one, and a little one which just held a gill. I would go down there, black dark, no lights, past Mahogany Row to the farm, and on the portico there would be an oil lamp and a box of matches. I would take the oil lamp, go into the byre, and milk Daisy and Bluebell, but not the others because they tended to kick. I'd take the bucket of milk into the dairy, put it through the separator, fill the cans, shout the farmer and his wife up, and the two sons, and go home. I used to drink out of the little can, between the lid, on my way home, drink this warm milk, and I often wondered why my mother never asked me why was there no milk left in the little can. Years after, I found she'd realised what I was doing, and it was the only way they knew I had drank any milk, because I really do detest it!

Ethel Murray

Beamish Hall Dairy

Beamish Hall had their own dairy, it was very new and very modern, it must have been built specially as a dairy, it was all beautiful. The basins they were polished tin, they didn't have chrome in those days. We used to love to go up there on a Sunday afternoon with the housemaid, maybe the kitchen maid – we'd go for eggs and butter or just for a walk. It was nice to see the milk going in the separating machine. There was the two spouts, the solid cream came out thick – we used to love to take a teaspoon with us and pinch the cream. And the milk that came through was just like blue water you know, it wasn't much use, but

Bill Jones milking a cow at High Hamsterley Farm, *c.* 1952.

it went to feeding hens and all those sorts of things. But the milk we used was perfect, and the butter was lovely, we made all our own butter.

Minnie Arbuckle

Watery Milk

Jenny Golden's family couldn't afford milk. Isaac Golden worked at the colliery and they had a lot of bairns. They used to use that Fussels skimmed milk in the tin. We used to go for Mrs Mitford who lived over the road, for milk. But we used to drink the milk, and fill it up at the horse trough, Jenny and I. Till she got a bit greedy and drank too much, made it too watery, and Mrs Mitford came over and said, 'I'm going to stop that milk at Potts … what was yours like?' I said, 'Aye, it has been a bit watery these days!' So I got a good hiding, a good clip. That trough is still there …

Doreen Scarrat

Potato Picking

And you used to get the tatie picking in the October, that was hard work, nearly as hard as pit work. What happens is, you used to go to the top farm, see Mr Oxley. There would be women and men, and lads like myself. He would look at you, and say, 'Why, I think he's strong for to tatie pick, stand at one side' and 'You've got a job, stand there' or 'You're no good, you can go home.' You had a stretch of maybe ten yards, that was your stretch, putting the potatoes in the pails, filling the bags, get right to the end, turn around, and back again. Hard work.

Then when the field was finished they used to run over it with the chain harrows, and all the taties what hadn't been picked, what had been stamped into the ground, that was fetching them all up. So you had to follow the tractors, picking them all up. But you did it, because you were trying to bring money into the house, like. And he used to pay the women more than what the men got. Well they must have thought, women that's coming out here to tatie pick, they must be the breadwinners of the house, so we'll give them extra.

Derek Hall

No Men Available

At Pockerley we had a lad who used to live in, to do the farm work, and there was a girl who used to live in and help with the housework. And the farmer used to get women or girls to do the outside work – hoeing turnips and potatoes and harvesting and such like. Because, you see, during the war most of the men

Women and children pick potatoes in the wake of a tractor. This photo was taken near Rowland's Gill, *c.* 1952.

A group of farm workers by a haystack.

had been called up, and there was no men available. There used to be some that worked in the collieries, and if they fancied it when they finished the shift, they used to come and help at hay time with the harvest.

Mr and Miss Bell

Leading the Horse

I'd take holidays and weekends to help on the farm. It was all manual work. When they were stacking, the hay had to be hand-forked up, and then the first thing you got was a horse pole, a big pole, and a horse pulled it up and then backed it back to drop the hay on top of the stack. That was a job I used to have, leading this horse backwards and forwards. From the lower portion of the farm, it was a very heavy pull up to the top of the farmyard. At night it always required two horses, there was a trace horse going backwards and forwards. You got your food when you were there, and maybe got a couple of rabbits to take home or that sort of thing, you never dreamed about pay.

Jack Geddes

Driving the Reaper

The reaper had two seats on. One of course for the driver of the reaper, and the other one was where my father used to sit, right over where the shears were going backwards and forwards. As it cut the corn he wanted it to fall backwards rather than forwards. He would have a big sort of elongated rake affair knocking it back and then the womenfolk would follow behind and gather all this corn that had been knocked down into certain sized bundles, and then tie it with string to make stooks.

Ernie Cheeseman

Horse Medicine

For ringworm, on horses and cattle, you used to use black sulphur and oil, and paint it onto the ringworm – it killed them so they didn't spread. Later than that, for ringworm on cattle, you used to get a drop of petrol and drop petrol on to kill them. For colic in horses, you used to mix pepper and mint and put it on their tongue, and let them lick: that cured colic provided you caught them in time. And for thrush in horses' feet, you used to get blue vitriol and water and put it in, or butter of antimony. It was a liquid; you could see it burning and give the gases off. It didn't hurt the horse, it helped it with being lame, it cured it. And we used to use Stockholm tar and salt for curing foot and mouth. You put it on the tongue, let them lick it in, and it cleared the sores on the mouth, got into the bloodstream, to purify it. And you put a little bit of Stockholm tar where they were sore.

Mr Bell

Sheep being driven along the road at New Acres Farm, Quaking Houses, towards South Moor, August 1935. (*Durham Advertiser*)

Cattle Transport

On a butcher's Monday we used to go on the twenty to twelve train to Newcastle. Then we used to walk from Central Station to the cattle market, and we used to walk them out the town, the sheep and the beast. Used to get a shilling a piece for beast and tuppence a piece for sheep. It would take about three hours, easy. Sometimes the beast used to lie down. It was canny but it was a long walk, in hot weather it was terrible, terrible. And it was terrible in the winter time especially.

Syd Wears

Travelling Goose Seller

A chap used to walk geese from village to village, getting near Christmas time, selling the geese around the farms. If a field had been a cornfield, he would go and see the farmer – they used to eat among the stubble, get all the corn out – and so the farmer would say, 'Oh, I'll have a dozen or so,' or maybe only half a dozen. This chap would have a hundred when he started – you would hear them, 'quack, quack, quack', walking along the road. I used to see them when I was a lad, see them coming around.

Jack Edgell

Allotments

We didn't have an allotment, simply because my father did not like gardening – I think we were about the only men in South Moor that didn't. My wife's father was a very keen gardener and had two brothers who were also keen gardeners – there were four allotments going with that lot. They had wonderful asparagus out of the garden, mind you it was seasonal. And potatoes and what have you.

Ernie Cheeseman

The Beamish Show

The colliery used to make a barrow every year for the Beamish Show; it was held at the Shepherd and Shepherdess. The colliery supplied a barrow for the pitmen, that was one of the prizes, a wheelbarrow, and it was made at Beamish Yard, you see. These shows used to show everything, flowers as well, and leeks. But in olden days it was just the show, Beamish Show.

Jack Edgell

The *Durham Advertiser* captured this image of men proudly displaying their prize leeks at the Stanley Show in 1952.

Christmas Greens

The woodman would cut a lot of holly and greenery, ivies and spruce, and then a cartload would be dumped in the back lane, people used to just go and take what they required, to decorate their homes for Christmas. They would have permission you see. And if a tree was blown down or they were felling trees, a horse and cart would come and tip a whole load of logs. But people weren't greedy, they took what they wanted and there was always enough.

Ethel Murray

Wood Cutting

I worked in a wood during the first war, taking trees to Rowlands Gill Station for them to gan to Newcastle. I had three horses and a wood wagon, and I used to be on the lead with the horse, or sitting on its back, ganning away through the wood. I was fetching six to eight trees out, there's some weight there. When we got to the station yard, they always had a crane in the station to lift the tree out and we would steady it down onto the wagon. There used to be an old man at that side, and me this side, get a hold of it and fetch it down, and then fasten them down with chains. Tight. They wouldn't move.

Joseph French

German Prisoners of War

The German prisoners thinned the wood out in Langley Moor Wood. They were chopping the trees down, chopping them into eight-foot lengths, for the drift, to timber the coal face and that up – props for the pit. They used to bring the prisoners from Hamsterley in the morning. As kids we used to go and watch them. This particular morning they were lobbing the branches off this tree and the German prisoner put the axe right up his leg there; he was never seen again, that one. I don't know if he died.

Derek Hall

Rat Catching

I've spent a long time rat catching by hand. How I found that out was simply by studying the rats. They made holes so that if anybody disturbed them when they were feeding on the ash tips, they ran into these holes until the danger went away. I found out that if I went down and pushed a tin in each of them holes … they would scream wild because I'd fastened them in. I would take the side of the tin away, allow one to put its head out and I would put my fingers on the back of its neck, a tight grip, and I could lift it out with my hand. Well it started a hobby and people got to know – some of my friends had seen me doing it. They started to come down with dogs and asked me if I would take these live rats to the top of the tip and release them so the dogs could go after them you see. And I said I would. As soon as I put the rat on the ground, the dogs were all set and the men were ready holding the dogs … gosh the dogs would go on there. And it was fascinating to see them dogs pacing them rats in and out like that – through the hedges, along the hedges. Well it became a weekly event and that went on for several months until I'd cleaned the place out of rats.

Samuel Jackson

Gun Clubs

My father kept pigs at the Shepherd and Shepherdess. One time when he went across to feed the pigs he saw some young rats, so he put a lump of meal down every morning – there was more and more every time he went. He did it on purpose because he was a gun man, he was in the gun club. He'd go and shoot with the Beamish Hall shooters when they had a gun party, and if the gentlemen was there he used to go as a loader, load their guns. After he put the meal down he got a big muster there, he got his double-barrelled gun out, and he killed twenty-two with the two shots. They had a gun club at the Shepherd

A group of men outside the Shepherd and Shepherdess pub, Beamish.

and Shepherdess, and there's a field close too – they had shooting matches in that field. One time when they were shooting the barrel exploded and blew a chap's fingers off – that finished the shooting for the day.

Jack Edgell

Crow Pie

We used to eat crows. My dad used to shoot them at the wood by the Shepherd and Shepherdess. There were a lot of rooks in there nesting before the leaves came on, and the young pop out before the leaves. My dad used to go shooting the rooks, and we used to go and pick them up. And my mother would make a crow pie, maybe six or eight in a pie. And my dad would shoot a rabbit. You would come back covered in blood.

Eddie Nicholson

If you enjoyed this book, you may also be interested in ...

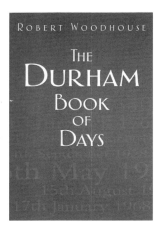

The Durham Book of Days

ROBERT WOODHOUSE

Taking you through the year day by day, *The Durham Book of Days* contains a quirky, eccentric, amusing and important events and facts from different periods of Durham's history. Ideal for dipping into, this addictive little book will keep you entertained and informed. Featuring hundreds of snippets of information gleaned from the vaults of Durham's archives, it will delight residents and visitors alike.

978 0 7524 7647 6

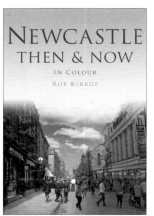

Newcastle Then & Now

ROB KIRKUP

Contrasting a selection of forty-five archive images alongside modern photographs taken from the same location, this new book reveals the changing faces, buildings and streets of Newcastle during the last century. Comparing the workers of yesteryear with today's trades-people, along with some famous landmarks and little-known street scenes, this is a wide-ranging look at the city's absorbing history.

978 0 7524 6566 1

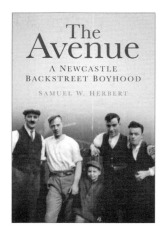

The Avenue: A Newcastle Backstreet Boyhood

SAMUEL W. HERBERT

Samuel Herbert had to grow up fast when his mother moves the family to a cockroach-infested tenement in Elswick while his dad – a miner – is away fighting on the front line. Along with the shared 'netties' and the terrible living conditions, Samuel learns how to deal with the bullies and the gangs until he grows as tough as they are. Along with the tragedy, however, came lots of laughs, and Samuel's unique account demonstrates the humour, courage and indomitable spirit of the local population. Prepare to be amused and entertained, surprised and moved by these stories, which vividly capture the heart and heritage of this former mining community.

978 0 7524 6886 0